A Big Ticket

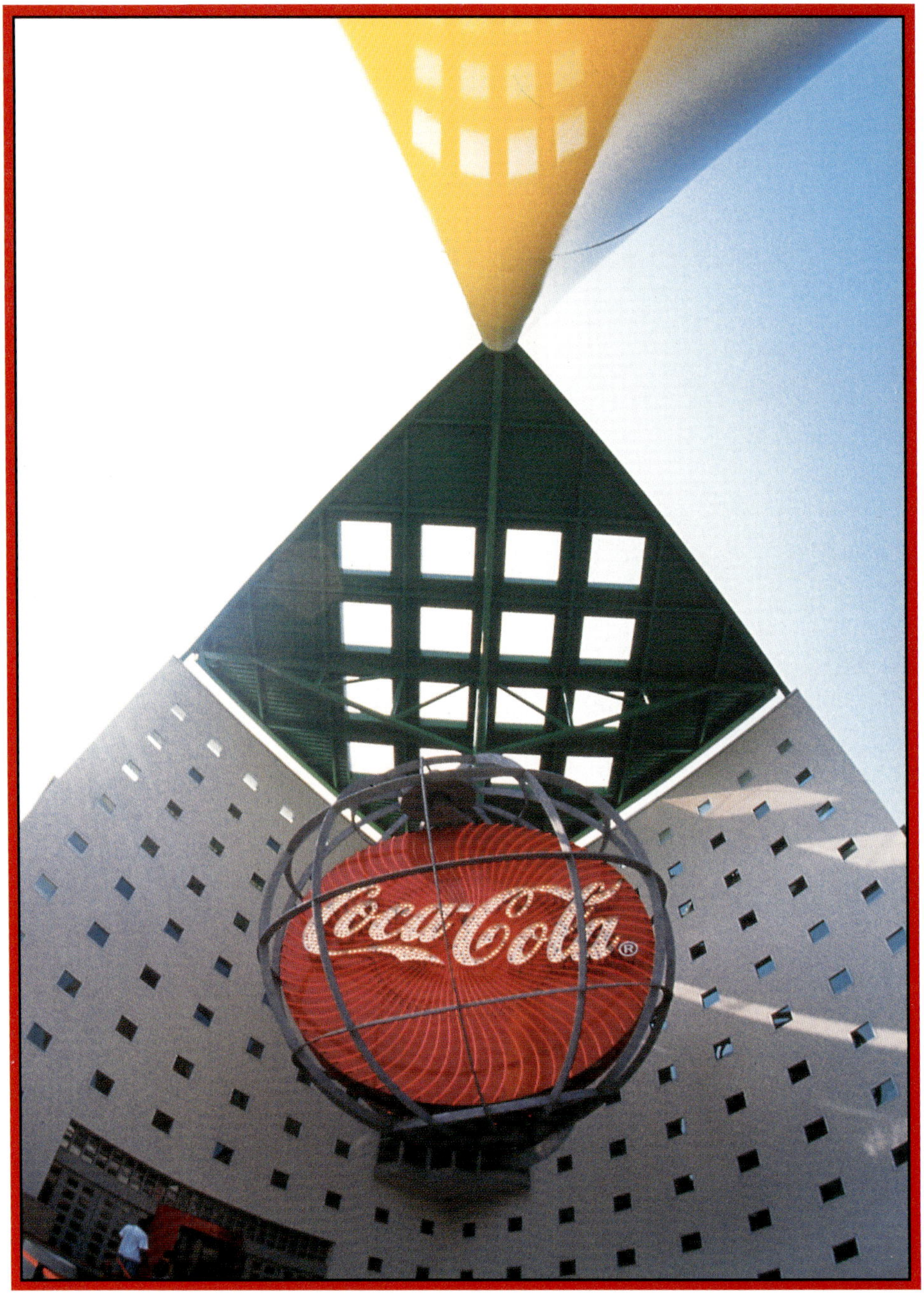
Coca-Cola

A Big Ticket

SPORTS and COMMERCIALISM

EVALEEN HU

Lerner Publications Company • Minneapolis

For my friends

On page 2: Workers raise an elaborate logo over the Coca-Cola museum that opened in Atlanta, site of the 1996 Olympics, shortly before the Games were held. Atlanta-based Coca-Cola was a major sponsor of the Olympics.

Copyright © 1998 by Lerner Publications Company

All rights reserved. International copyright secured.
No part of this book may be reproduced or transmitted in any form or by any means, electronic or mechanical, including photocopying and recording, or by any information storage or retrieval system, without permission in writing from Lerner Publications Company, except for the inclusion of brief quotations in an acknowledged review.

Website address: www.lernerbooks.com

Library of Congress Cataloging-in-Publication Data

Hu, Evaleen.
   A big ticket : sports and commercialism / by Evaleen Hu.
    p. cm.
   Includes bibliographical references (p.) and index.
   Summary: Discusses the commercial aspects of professional sports, examining endorsement contracts, sponsorship, broadcasting rights, salaries, agents, and more.
   ISBN 0–8225–3305–7 (alk. paper)
   1. Sports—United States—Marketing—Juvenile literature.
2. Sports—Economic aspects—United States—Juvenile literature.
[1. Professional sports—Marketing. 2. Professional sports—Economic aspects. 3. Sports—Marketing. 4. Sports—Economic aspects.] I. Title.
GV716.H8 1997
338.4'3796—dc20
                                                 96–40984

Manufactured in the United States of America
1 2 3 4 5 6 – JR – 02 01 00 99 98 97

CONTENTS

1 **A Front-Row Seat** 7
 Terms of the Trade. *21*
2 **Dollar Signs** 25
3 **Growth Spurt**. 41
4 **Selling Stars** 55
5 **Amateurs No More**. 73
 Notes *88*
 Bibliography *90*
 Index *94*

6 A BIG TICKET

CHAPTER ONE

A FRONT-ROW SEAT

Americans love watching sports. Television channels such as ESPN and The Sports Network broadcast games and sports news 24 hours a day. The Super Bowl is one of the most popular television events of the year, drawing more viewers than almost any other program. Basketball superstar Michael Jordan is among the most famous people on the planet.

Sports such as baseball, football, and basketball provide an escape from day-to-day life to a world of heroes, competition, drama, and excitement. But underneath the glamour and emotion, sports is also a business. Star athletes are paid millions of dollars. TV networks pay millions for the rights to broadcast games. Cities compete for professional teams with promises of tax breaks and new stadiums.

The sports marketplace is a complicated one. At the core are players, team owners, and event promoters such as the International Olympic Committee and the Professional Golfers' Association. They supply the entertainment and compete with each other for spectators' money and attention.

A BIG TICKET

In the early days of sports, owners relied on fans for most of the money taken in by a team. Over time, advertisers, television networks, and other businesses became the major sources of revenue.

Between the teams and the audience is another layer of businesses: television networks that broadcast games; advertisers, or sponsors, that pay networks to air commercials during televised events; sporting goods companies that hire athletes to promote their products; companies that sell mugs, hats, and T-shirts displaying team names and mascots.

These businesses also rely on sports fans for their success. Whether buying a ticket for a seat in a stadium, snatching up the latest basketball shoes, or watching a game on television, spectators supply the money that keeps the sports industry thriving.

Big-league sports weren't always so complicated. In the 1940s, for instance, major league teams were popular but not widespread. In baseball, 16 teams made up the major leagues, and most of them were in the East. The National Hockey League had only six teams. The National Football League and the National Basketball Association were still fledgling organizations. Fans listened to games on radios and read about sports heroes in the newspapers.

Then something happened that fueled a growth in professional sports and changed the industry forever. At the end of the 1940s, more and more Americans began to buy a new device: a television.

THE TV REVOLUTION

May 17, 1939: Princeton plays Columbia. The 10-inning baseball game would determine which team would take fourth place in the Ivy League standings. Princeton versus Columbia wasn't a watershed game in the history of sports. But it was a landmark for broadcasting. It was the first televised sporting event.

Hundreds gathered at the RCA Building in New York City to watch the event on a small black-and-white television set. Later, viewers would say that the players

Television coverage of sports events brings the action to a large audience.

looked like "white flies" on the screen. Announcer Bill Stern narrated, and the one camera provided a view of the infield. When the ball left the diamond, it also left the screen. Princeton won the game, 2–1.

Fast-forward to the late 1990s. Switch on the television on a Sunday afternoon in fall, and you'll probably find a pro football game. Announcers and often a former athlete or two will provide commentary on the game. Television cameras spread around the field will capture up-close views that most spectators at the stadium can't even see. If you miss a play, instant replay can show you what just happened—in slow motion. On-screen graphics will keep you updated on the score, statistics, and what's happening in other games across the country.

At the 1939 Princeton–Columbia game, few people would have predicted that the marriage of television and sports would last so long. And few would have predicted that television would have such a great impact on sports. "There have been comparable times in history when sports have been at the center of a culture and seemed to dominate the landscape. Whether in Greek society or in what used to be called the Golden Age of Sports. But everything is magnified by television," said Roone Arledge, former president of ABC Sports.[1]

The relationship between sports and television is a long story of give-and-take, of networks and leagues working together to make watching a game on TV as exciting as being right there. Indeed, sports broadcasting has come a long way since the Princeton–Columbia game.

THE BEST SEAT IN THE HOUSE

At first, team owners thought showing sports on television was foolish. They felt attracting fans to games was the best way to earn money and worried that televising games would bring fewer people through the turnstiles. The best seat for a game should be in the ballpark, they said.

But as more families bought televisions in the 1950s, the potential of sports on TV became harder to ignore. The number of television-watching families grew rapidly. In 1949, less than a million households had a television. By the mid-1950s, that number was more than 32 million.

No other medium could rival television in capturing the immediacy and action of sports. Unlike newspapers, books, magazines, or radio, television brought words and moving pictures together into viewers' living rooms. The action was live—broadcast as it happened.

In some cases, as critics had predicted, there was a negative impact on ticket sales. Minor league baseball is perhaps the best example. As networks began to show baseball games, spectators found fewer reasons to go to the local ballpark, especially when they could watch major league games from home. In 1947, 42 million spectators attended minor league games. By 1960, that number had fallen below 15 million.

BETTER PACKAGING

The success of televised sports comes largely from the vision of one man: ABC's Roone Arledge. He realized early on that sports were perfect for television, and his ideas on how to show games changed sports broadcasting forever. In a famous memo to ABC executives in 1961, Arledge detailed exactly how he would transform the network. His ideas were unheard of: He envisioned instant replays, extensive Olympic coverage, sophisticated on-screen graphics, underwater cameras, and evening football games.

By the time Arledge joined ABC to produce sports in 1960, he already knew the ins and outs of television. But his task at the network would be difficult. Other networks already covered the most popular sporting events. NBC had Friday night boxing. CBS had the Kentucky Derby and pro football and baseball.

Arledge pushed on, and under his leadership, ABC beefed up its

Roone Arledge

A BIG TICKET

sports offerings. It bought rights to televise National Collegiate Athletic Association (NCAA) football games and created *Wide World of Sports,* a show that presented golf, tennis, the Olympics, and more offbeat events such as cliff diving from Acapulco.

The rule at *Wide World of Sports,* which made its debut on April 29, 1961, was to show anything, as long as you made it interesting for the audience. With an eye for quality and drama—and sometimes stretching the definition of "sport"—the program

Wide World of Sports gives fans a chance to watch exciting, but less popular, competitions like alpine skiing.

set the standard for sports broadcasting and whetted Americans' appetite for sports of all kinds.

International sporting events such as the Olympics were particularly popular. Interest was fueled by the Cold War, a period of hostility between the United States and the Soviet Union. "It became apparent with the Olympics in those days that if you had an American against a Russian, it didn't matter what they were doing, they could have been kayaking and people would watch it," Roone Arledge said.[2]

FOOTBALL GOES PRIME TIME

Wide World of Sports, still on the air after more than 3½ decades, became the longest-running sports series. And it was profitable. But ABC's big moneymaker was *Monday Night Football,* which premiered in 1970. Before *Monday Night Football,* most games were shown on Sunday afternoons. Many TV executives thought broadcasting football during prime time—the peak evening hours of television viewing—was a bad idea: Audiences wouldn't choose football over other popular shows, critics said.

Before the Olympics became a coveted (and high-priced) television event, fans would watch coverage of such highlights as Bob Beamon's record-shattering long jump on ABC's *Wide World of Sports.*

A BIG TICKET

THE TV TICKET

Pay-per-view could be the wave of the future for televised sports. Here's how pay-per-view works: Viewers with access to cable television call their cable companies and arrange to watch a premier sporting event for a price. Only those who pay—either the pay-per-view fee or for an actual ticket—can watch the event.

Pay-per-view has its pros and cons. When the Minnesota North Stars hockey team made home playoff games available only on pay-per-view in 1991, it outraged fans. But enough viewers paid the $12.95-per-game fee to make the games extremely profitable. A 1988 bout between Mike Tyson and Michael Spinks brought in $21 million in pay-per-view income. NBC's pay-per-view coverage of parts of the 1992 Olympics, on the other hand, was a massive financial failure.

Pay-per-view also has its critics. Because boxing is shown almost exclusively on pay-per-view, critics say that novice viewers are less likely to develop an interest in the sport. And since only top boxing events are televised, low- to mid-level fights might go unnoticed.

"The sport is certainly not as robust as it was," said boxing promoter Bob Arum. "Boxing hasn't done enough to attract younger viewers and younger customers. One reason for that is the sport went from being on network television to closed-circuit and pay-per-view."

Source: Reingold, Jennifer. "Thriving on Chaos: Boxing Still Commands Big Bucks, But the Power is Concentrated in Fewer Hands." *Financial World*, 14 February 1995.

SPORTS AND COMMERCIALISM 15

Would boxing attract more fans if bouts were televised on network television?

A BIG TICKET

The immediate success of prime-time football proved the critics wrong—and everyone benefited. Advertisers had their messages seen by a large audience; ABC got good ratings and could sell advertising time at high prime-time prices; fans got to see football at night.

Monday Night Football also made watching a game more entertaining. Using slow-motion instant replays and on-screen graphics, the show gave viewers

Don Meredith, Howard Cosell, and Frank Gifford were the broadcast team that drew a phenomenal number of viewers to tune in to *Monday Night Football.*

Superstars like quarterback Joe Namath helped make the NFL popular with fans—and television broadcasters loved the large audience.

more information than fans got in the stadium. Opinionated announcer Howard Cosell provided color commentary, outraging some viewers and amusing others. The country became caught up in football, fueled by Cosell's critical narration. This interest translated into ratings, the television industry's measure of a show's popularity. By the fall of 1971, *Monday Night Football* was attracting 30 million viewers each week.

The success of *Monday Night Football* sparked bidding wars for the rights to broadcast football games. All the networks wanted a piece of the action. NFL commissioner Pete Rozelle took advantage of football's popularity, and the NFL profited. In 1977, the

A BIG TICKET

league's contracts with the networks yielded $656 million over four years. By 1993, the four-year figure would rise to include the $1.6 billion the Fox network paid to televise National Football Conference games.

MADE FOR TELEVISION

Television poured billions of dollars into the football leagues' pockets and enhanced the game by providing a view of the action that most spectators in stadiums had to squint to see. In turn, football delivered high ratings and a young male audience to the networks.

As televisions became bigger and color television became the norm, football teams changed the color and design of uniforms to make names, numbers, and logos more visible to cameras. The league agreed to commercial time-outs—breaks in play just so advertisements could be shown.

Other sports were quick to imitate football's success. Industry leaders recognized that television could deliver wealth and changed their games to suit television's needs. Tennis officials speeded up their game and created a tiebreaker rule to make the matches more

SPORTS AND COMMERCIALISM | **19**

In exchange for all the money they spend on the rights to broadcast games, networks have adapted aspects of the competitions to meet their needs.

A BIG TICKET

exciting for TV audiences. Not long after *Monday Night Football* debuted, baseball owners moved most games from daytime to prime time.

Seasons were lengthened to give teams, networks, and advertisers more opportunities to make money. The basketball season expanded, spreading out from its traditional winter months into fall and late spring. The Winter and Summer Olympics used to be held in the same year. Beginning in 1994, the Summer and Winter Games began alternating every two years—to balance out the sale of television advertising time.

SUPER BOWL, SUPER PROFITS

The Super Bowl remains the crown jewel in broadcasting. Almost a cultural event in the United States, the Super Bowl is often the most-watched television show of the year. Games are among the highest-rated in television history. Because of the almost guaranteed high ratings, networks stand to make a lot of money from advertisers during the Super Bowl. Games start in the early evening, and commercials are sold at costly prime-time

The Super Bowl is an extravagant affair.

TERMS OF THE TRADE

agent: A business representative who works for an athlete, negotiating contracts, endorsement deals, and other financial agreements.

broadcasting rights or **television rights:** An agreement between a television network and a team, league, or association that allows the network to tape and broadcast sporting events.

endorsement: Promotion of a product or company. Athletes frequently promote companies by using their products or appearing in their advertisements.

free agent: An athlete who is free to negotiate a contract with any team.

merchandising rights or **licensing:** An agreement between a manufacturer and a team, league, or association that allows the manufacturer to make and sell clothing and souvenirs bearing team names and logos.

reserve system: A system by which professional athletes were bound to their teams until retirement, release, or a trade.

salary cap: A limit on the dollar amount professional leagues will allow each team to spend on all of its player salaries combined.

sponsor: A business that provides money to an athlete, team, network, or event in exchange for endorsements or advertising.

A BIG TICKET

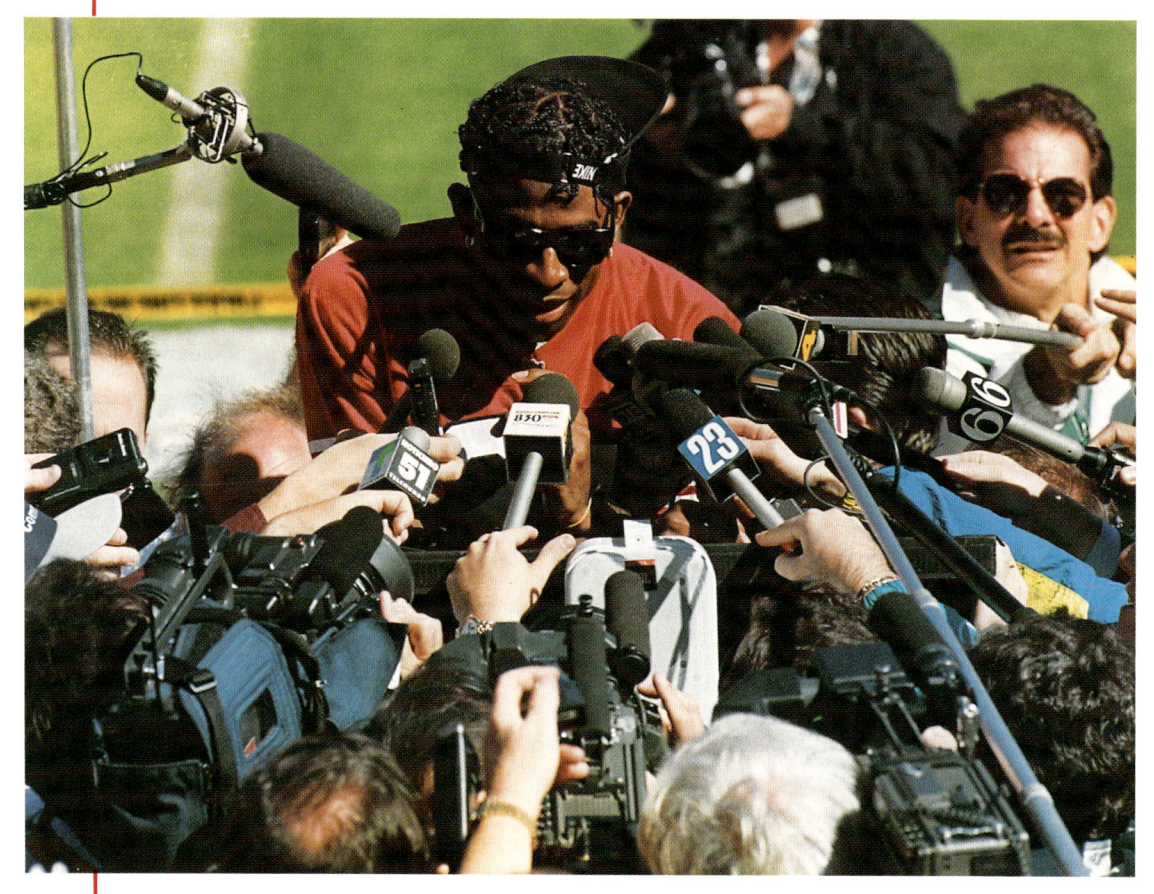

Hordes of reporters and photographers surround Super Bowl players in the weeks leading up to the game, contributing to the pre-game buildup.

rates. During the 1991 Super Bowl, ABC charged as much as $875,000 for 30 seconds of advertising time.

Is the high price worth it for advertisers? Apparently so. The television audience is so large that the Master Lock Company spent a year's advertising budget to air just one commercial during the Super Bowl. For sporting goods companies such as Nike, exposure during a major sporting event is invaluable. "The Super Bowl is the most watched sports event of the year, and as a company that made a name for itself in sports and fitness, it's very important to us," said Thomas E. Clarke, vice president of marketing at Nike.[3]

Indeed, the commercials have taken a life of their own. Many advertisers launch new campaigns during the Super Bowl, and, after the game, viewers debate which commercial was the best. The game's halftime show, too, is planned as a spectacular affair, with big-name entertainers, to keep viewers tuned to the event—and to the halftime commercials.

Under the watchful eye of the television cameras, the sports industry has ballooned into a multibillion-dollar enterprise. Teams now depend heavily on selling television rights. Without TV, there would be few viewers and even fewer commercial sponsors. Without TV, teams wouldn't have the money they need to pay players' ever-growing salaries.

24 A BIG TICKET

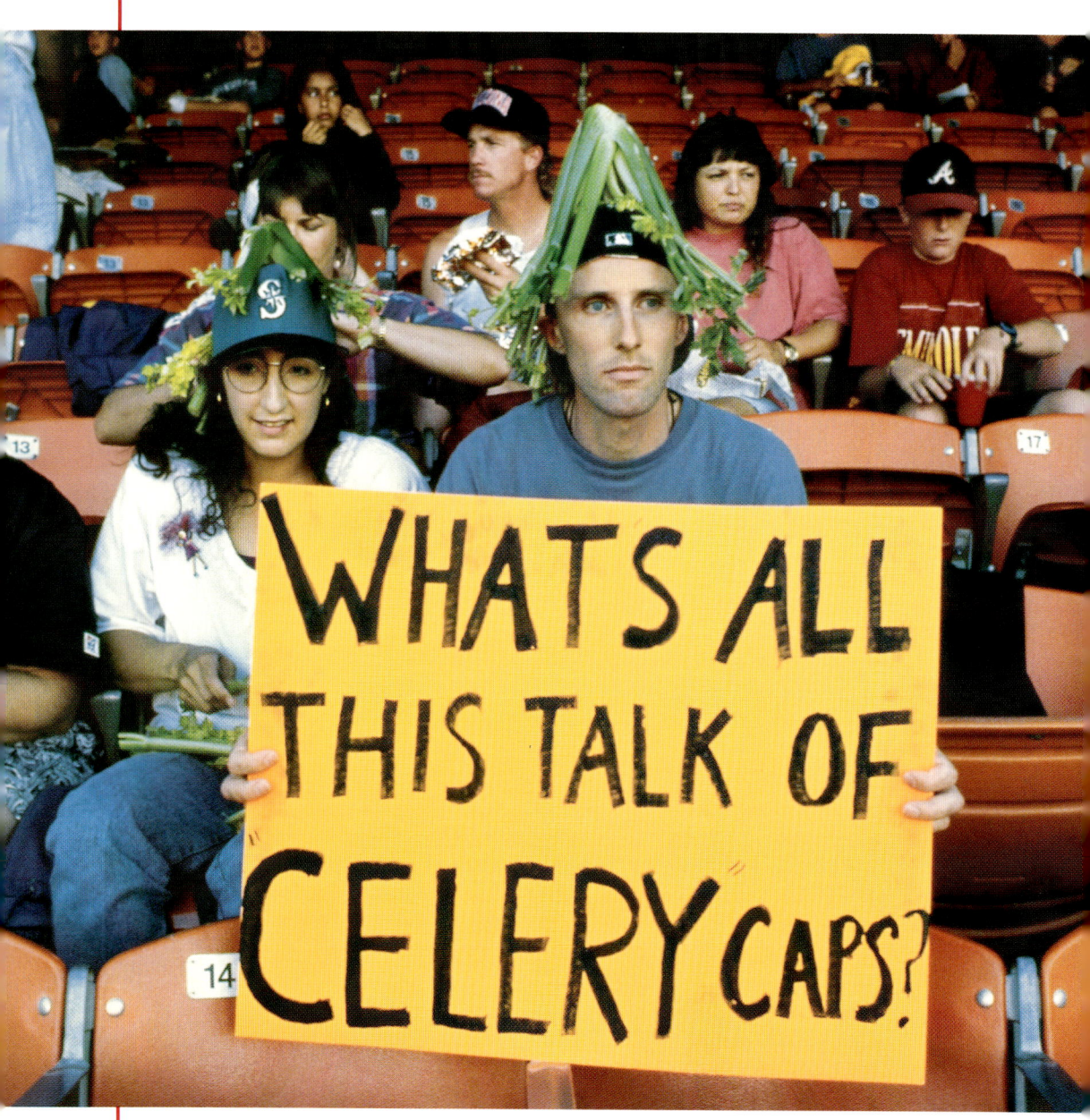

WHAT'S ALL THIS TALK OF CELERY CAPS?

Sports fans who believe players and team owners already make plenty of money have little sympathy for labor disputes between the two sides.

CHAPTER TWO

DOLLAR SIGNS

When Roger Bannister ran the first four-minute mile in 1954, he set a world record but wasn't paid anything for his feat. In recent years, track star Carl Lewis has earned thousands of dollars just for showing up at meets. In 1973, baseball players on average earned $36,566. By 1994, the average salary in baseball was $1.2 million. Top players such as Bobby Bonilla earned more than $6 million a year.

Everywhere you look in professional sports, athletes are earning more money for doing the same thing their predecessors did: entertaining spectators. Critics say high-paid athletes no longer embody old-fashioned ideals such as hard work, teamwork, and love of the game. "When I was playing, you weren't going to make a whole lot of money," said football great Jim Brown, who played in the 1950s and 1960s. "But you were playing the game, and playing the game at the highest possible level. And you liked that."[1]

"The basic ill in sports today has got to be money and it's ultimately going to corrupt everything," says Roone Arledge. "You have owners who can't control themselves giving all this money to players. You have 25-year-old kids making several million dollars a year and thinking they're entitled to it: They argue that rock stars and movie stars make that kind of money, and they're performers just like athletes are. But I would like to think there's a difference between an athlete and a rock star. Unfortunately, it may well be that as new generations come along, they won't miss the virtues that used to be at the center of sport."[2]

THE FREE AGENT REVOLUTION

Free agency, a player's right to sell his services to any team he wants, changed the way professional sports teams did business. Before free agency, most major league sports operated under the reserve system: Owners decided whether to keep or trade players. Athletes didn't choose their teams. Salaries were relatively low.

Owners opposed free agency, arguing that restricting a player's freedom was good for business. If free agency were allowed in its purest form, owners said, bidding for players would go so high that some teams might go out of business. Only wealthy clubs would be able to afford star athletes, leaving poorer teams with lesser athletes. Lack of real competition would cause fans to lose interest, hurting the leagues and the players.

Athletes argued that they deserved to choose their employer, just like other workers do. They also said they should draw high salaries because they were the ones who attracted fans. The players' fight for free agency started with St. Louis Cardinal Curt Flood in 1969. The Cardinals had traded the 12-year veteran to Philadelphia, but he refused to go.

Curt Flood

"I do not feel that I am a piece of property to be bought and sold,"[3] Flood wrote to commissioner Bowie Kuhn. Flood went to court, charging Major League Baseball with violating anti-trust laws meant to keep businesses from tightly controlling their markets. He lost his case, but other players and the players' union continued the fight.

In 1975, the reserve system was struck down when Andy Messersmith and Dave McNally won requests to be freed from their clubs. From then on, players with experience in the major leagues could offer their services to the highest bidder.

Still, the courts acknowledged that pure free agency would strain the game. So owners and players compromised. Owners agreed to give players some movement between teams, and players agreed to have some restrictions put on them. The new system has built-in limitations, such as the draft, in which teams get to choose new players.

On November 4, 1976, 30 free agents put themselves on the

Andy Messersmith

Dave McNally

A BIG TICKET

market. Baltimore Oriole Reggie Jackson was the hottest ticket. Thirteen teams lined up to sign him. He agreed to join the New York Yankees for $2.9 million over five years and became the highest-paid player in the game. The average salary for baseball players rose from $51,501 to $76,066 that season. By 1994, the figure was $1.2 million.

FREE AGENCY IN FOOTBALL

Unrestricted free agency didn't exist in football until January 6, 1993, when players and owners signed a seven-year agreement. Under the agreement, all players with five years in the league and an expired contract could become free agents.

To keep teams competitive and payrolls from skyrocketing out of control, the agreement included a salary cap, a limit on how much each club could spend on all player salaries, bonuses, and incentives combined. The salary cap would keep wealthier teams from getting all the superstars and help small-market owners control their costs.

In the first season of free agency, in 1994, the bidding for top players reached a frenzy. More

Reggie Jackson was all smiles when he signed with the Yankees in 1976.

Quarterback Terry Bradshaw stayed with the Pittsburgh Steelers for his whole NFL career—and won four Super Bowls.

than one-third of the league's quarterbacks switched teams. Not so long ago, players such as the Pittsburgh Steelers' Terry Bradshaw stayed with a team for their entire careers. They worked to build up their teams and to foster loyalty among fans. With free agency in football, loyalty took a back seat. The mass migration in the NFL sent a clear signal to fans, owners, and players that a new era had arrived.

Even average players put themselves on the market and shopped around for a bigger salary. "Without a good supporting cast, your superstar can't perform at his highest level, so the value of many of those midlevel players will increase,"[4] said Lynn Swann, former wide receiver for the Pittsburgh Steelers. With salaries of every player increasing, some teams found they couldn't afford to keep their stars.

A BIG TICKET

Quarterback Phil Simms, a 15-year veteran with the New York Giants, was released before training camp began in 1994. The Giants shed his $2.5 million salary amid the staff's uncertainty about Simms's ability to come back from shoulder surgery and play effectively at age 38. Instead, the team turned to younger and less costly players like David Brown and Kent Graham to fill the quarterback spot.

Simms, who retired and took a job as commentator for ESPN, blamed his release on the new salary cap. The previous season, he had thrown for 3,000 yards and 15 touchdowns as the Giants went 12–4. Simms felt he could perform at the same level in 1994. When he had heard NFL commissioner Paul Tagliabue say again and again that the salary cap wouldn't force teams to dump players they wanted to keep, he

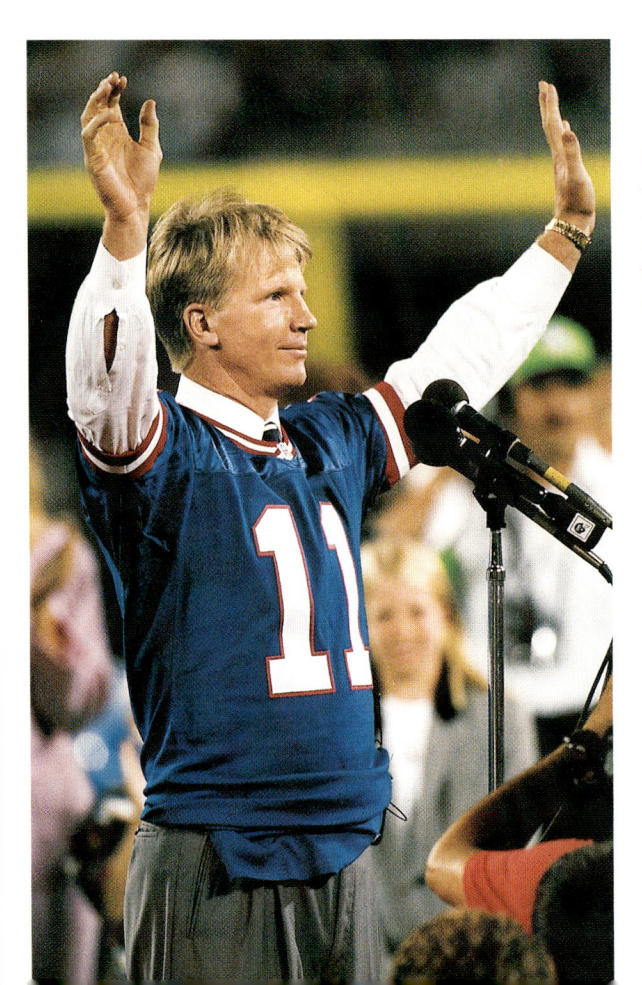

Longtime New York Giants quarterback Phil Simms retired when he was released by the team after the NFL salary cap took effect.

disagreed. "I was not let go because of the salary cap? That's one of the stupidest things I've ever heard,"[5] he said.

Perhaps the biggest switch of 1994 involved Warren Moon, quarterback for the Houston Oilers. The Oilers traded Moon to the Minnesota Vikings for two draft picks. The Oilers would have had to pay $3.25 million a year for the aging quarterback. Instead, the team opted for the younger Cody Carlson, who commanded a smaller paycheck.

At 37, Moon was still one the league's top quarterbacks, throwing for 21 touchdowns and 3,485 yards in the 1993 season. He was disappointed that he wouldn't be able to finish his career in Houston, where he had strong family and community ties. "I've given the Oilers every ounce of my effort for 10 years. Doesn't that mean anything?"[6] Moon said.

THE NBA'S SUCCESS

The National Basketball Association operated under the reserve system until 1975, when a court ruling brought the system to an end. The NBA and players then forged a new labor contract, allowing restricted free agency.

Warren Moon was disappointed when the Oilers traded him to make room under the salary cap.

BILLIE JEAN KING'S LEGACY

In the 1960s, tennis player Billie Jean King worked as a playground instructor at Los Angeles State College to pay her bills. In her free time, she served and volleyed her way to Grand Slam finals. After winning the singles title at Wimbledon in 1966, King took home a £50 voucher (worth about $140 in U.S. money) to go toward new tennis clothes.

In 1991, when Monica Seles was just 17 years old, she already had made tennis history as the youngest woman to be ranked number 1. She earned $1.5 million that year from tournament prizes alone. Her earnings off the court were four times that amount, thanks to endorsement deals with Perrier, Yonex, Canon, Fila, and Matrix.

How did tennis players get this far? Much of the explosion in money and celebrity is because of King, who organized female professionals and campaigned to bring prize money to women's tournaments. In 1971, King became the first woman to win $100,000 in a season. By the 1990s, prize money on the Women's Tennis Association tour totaled $35 million.

Billie Jean King won the Wimbledon platter, along with a £50 voucher in 1966.

SPORTS AND COMMERCIALISM 33

When the Los Angeles Lakers won the NBA title in 1987, the league was heathy again.

In 1983, NBA officials and players met again. The league was in deep financial trouble. Attendance at games was low, and television audiences showed little interest. Free agency had sent players' salaries into the stratosphere. Without drastic action, the league would have to cut the number of teams from 23 to 16.

This time, players and owners reached a revolutionary agreement: Players would always receive 53 percent of the league's revenues; owners, 47 percent. The players agreed to a salary cap, but the teams' salary caps would grow as the league grew, giving everyone a stake in the league's success.

"What made it happen in basketball was that the players and management were in the gutter together. Everyone saw how necessary it was for both sides to work together to survive,"[7] said Charles Grantham, head of the NBA Players Association.

Thanks to the landmark agreement, the NBA enjoyed a long period of harmony and prosperity. The league has been hailed as a model of sports management.

PROFITS AND PITFALLS

Team owners aren't happy about players' high paychecks. In baseball, owners say that players' high salaries are straining the teams, bringing them uncomfortably close to financial ruin. Players accuse owners of exaggerating their losses. Players and owners operated for more than two years without a basic agreement. This debate came to a head at the end of the 1994 baseball season. With seven weeks left to play, players went on strike rather than agree to the salary cap owners said was needed.

Young fans pleaded with players and owners to avoid a baseball strike in 1994. The strike occurred anyway, and the league canceled the World Series for the first time in 90 years. Diehard fans were furious.

SPORTS AND COMMERCIALISM

Baseball and football star Bo Jackson saw his sports careers end prematurely because of a football injury.

Athletes argue that they have only a short time to make money doing what they do best. In football, the average career lasts only 3½ years. And playing pro sports is full of pitfalls. One false move on artificial turf or a nasty case of tendinitis can end an athletic career. Because of the physical intensity of sports, many athletes live with nagging injuries for the rest of their lives. High salaries are insurance, they argue, against future medical bills, as well as the long years in which they're too old to earn a living in sports.

Bo Jackson was one of many athletes who saw his career come to a grinding halt due to injury. In 1991, Jackson was a two-sport sensation, earning more than $2.4 million doing double duty for baseball's Kansas City Royals and football's Los Angeles Raiders. He was also a popular pitchman. His success didn't last. On January 13, he injured his hip during a Raiders game, ending his career in football. He had hip-replacement surgery and eventually played baseball again—but never with the same success. In 1995, Bo left pro sports for good.

THE KEY TO WINNING

When Jackson was injured, a baseball team and a football team lost a valuable, though costly, player. Star athletes can make the difference on a team, but high-paid players aren't necessarily the key to winning. A team that works together, especially in a sport such as football, can save money and win the loyalty of fans.

In 1991, the San Diego Chargers let high-priced—but often selfish—talents leave town and replaced them with solid team players with smaller egos. The Chargers operated on the philosophy that teamwork is just as important as talent. "I don't want every player on my team to have a halo over his head. That's unrealistic. But I'd rather have good players who are good people than great players who are bad people. Sometimes you make decisions based on chemistry more than talent,"[8] said Bobby Ross, who coached the Chargers.

Owners have long contended that under free agency, wealthy teams would snatch up all the star players and consistently win championships. That hasn't been the case so far. For 16 years after free agency took effect, the New York Yankees were the only baseball team to win two championships in a row. In contrast, before free agency, the Yankees—especially from the 1920s to the 1960s—dominated the World Series.

AGENTS STEP IN

Higher salaries came with a slew of complications for athletes. All of a sudden, they needed to negotiate contracts with team owners. In school, most athletes aren't taught about contracts or negotiations. That's where agents come in. An athlete hires an agent to work out a deal that suits the athlete's interests, and the agent receives part of the money in return.

Agents play a key role for athletes, many of whom go from

poor college student to rich professional athlete overnight. An athlete's financial success often depends on which agent he or she chooses, and finding the right agent can be confusing. Competition is fierce among agents to represent players.

Long before draft day, student-athletes receive a flood of mail, phone calls, and attention. "We're even hearing stories of high school athletes getting sucked in by agents," says Richard Lapchick, director of Northeastern University's Center for the Study of Sport in Society. "They give the athletes money . . . anything to get them beholden to them."[9]

Tennis prodigy Venus Williams was only 13 when agents began swarming around her, eager to help her invest the millions of dollars in her future. "They see

By the time she was 13, tennis player Venus Williams seemed like such a sure bet to be a star that agents tried to persuade her to sign with them.

her as a dollar sign," said Venus's father, Richard. "We see her as a little girl. They don't want to sign Venus, they want to use her."[10]

With hundreds of agents courting them, athletes such as Williams must ask: Whom do I trust? "Do these kids have enough time to make a good decision? Well, they have to make time. They don't have a choice at this point,"[11] says agent John Maloney.

Very few programs are in place to protect young athletes from signing with bad agents. At Duke University, law school professors and university lawyers evaluate agents for players. Most other schools offer only tips on how to find the right agents.

An agent's services can vary. The agent might negotiate contracts, land endorsement deals, manage the athlete's taxes, or give spending allowances. Some athletes choose a large agency to handle their affairs. Many of these firms, such as International Management Group and Advantage International, provide all the services an individual agent does—and then some. When Alonzo Mourning joined the NBA in 1992, Nike Sports Management not only helped him select an agent to negotiate with the Charlotte Hornets, it also selected a townhouse for him and had parts of the dwelling customized for his height.

NCAA rules prohibit student-athletes from signing with agents and accepting money before their college careers end. But college sports have been filled with violations. In 1987, New York agent Norby Walters was accused of luring nearly 50 athletes to sign with

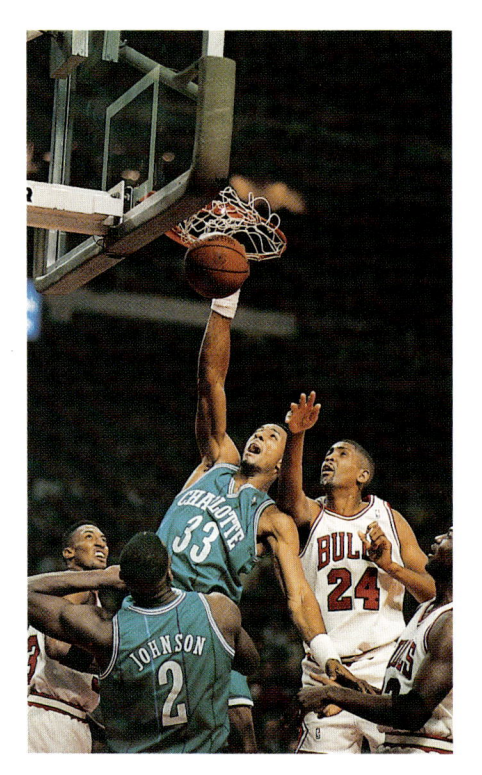

Alonzo Mourning had many of his personal deals arranged by agents.

SPORTS AND COMMERCIALISM

Athletes coming out of college, like Steve Young did in 1984, rely on their agents to make good business decisions for them. Young signed with Leigh Steinberg, who has become one of the top agents in the United States.

him while they were still eligible to play college ball. The players accepted money and lavish gifts from Walters.

The Norby Walters case exposed corruption among sports agents. There are no licenses, tests, or set requirements for agents in the industry. Anyone can hold the job. The NFL Players Association certifies agents, but certification involves only filling out an application, attending a seminar, and paying an annual fee.

Many agents have law degrees, but "there's no school you can go to to learn this business," says agent Steve Olschwanger. "You don't know what you're doing the first five years. Attorneys think they can fare better than a guy who is not an attorney. But there's no logic to this business. A person comes in and tries it—they get killed."[12]

How well the agent manages the player's money often determines how well the player lives after his or her career has ended. Good agents can make earnings from a short career last a lifetime. Bad agents can ruin an athlete.

A BIG TICKET

The Orlando Magic and the Toronto Raptors are two teams that have been added to the NBA since the mid-1980s.

CHAPTER THREE

GROWTH SPURT

Earlier in the century, sports leagues avoided expansion. Limiting the number of franchises, or teams, in a league meant more money for a small group of owners. With fewer teams, a single team could draw a bigger profit.

But as sports grew more popular through TV exposure, leagues and owners realized they could benefit by expanding into new markets. Expansion began cautiously in the 1960s. In baseball, the American League added teams in California and Washington. The National League expanded with teams in Houston and New York. The NFL added the Dallas Cowboys in 1960, followed by the Minnesota Vikings the next year. NBA expansion also began in 1960 with the Chicago Packers.

By the 1990s, all the leagues were growing—even outside their traditional geographic boundaries. The National Hockey League, with the vast majority of its teams in Canada and the northern United States, added teams in southern states like Texas, Florida, and California. The NBA had new teams in Canada. The NFL started the World League of American Football—with

A BIG TICKET

teams in the United States and overseas—to develop young players and, just as importantly, to create international interest in the largely North American sport.

BIDDING WARS

Having a professional sports team in town boosts residents' pride and can make a city more inviting to businesses and tourists. Some say losing a team can be financially devastating. If a team moves, restaurants, hotels, parking facilities, and other establishments that cater to fans often suffer. Local governments sometimes go to great lengths and costs to keep owners happy and attract new teams. City leaders often compete with one another to land an

NFL Commissioner Paul Tagliabue (right) announced that an expansion franchise had been granted for the Carolina Panthers, while the team's majority owner, Jerry Richardson, displayed a jersey.

Financing arrangements for new stadiums or tax breaks for the teams often determine whether a city can land pro sports franchises.

expansion team or lure existing teams away from other cities.

Because of such heavy competition, team owners can reap lavish benefits. They might threaten to move to another city if they don't get what they want—anything from a tax break to a new stadium. "The owners are playing a very cynical game with the people. It's the power of greed. The owners know they can blackmail city governments, which face political costs if the team moves,"[1] said Maryland Senator Howard Denis, whose state built a $70 million stadium for the Baltimore Orioles because owner Edward Bennett Williams was unhappy with Memorial Stadium.

Most new ballparks are built with taxpayers' money, a fact that

STADIUM SWEET STADIUM

Increasingly, owners of pro sports teams are looking for good stadium deals to maximize their profits. A key part of any deal is control of such things as the refreshments and souvenirs sold during games and other events, the advertising shown in a stadium, and high-priced luxury suites.

Whether or not they own the building, many teams have worked out an arrangement to prepare and sell all the snacks and beverages for their home games—and often for events unrelated to the team. The team will hire a company to manage the concessions and take a share of the money earned. More profit-minded owners such as the Dallas Cowboys' Jerry Jones have discovered that some companies, such as Pepsi-Cola, will pay to make sure their products are the only ones of the kind sold in the stadium. He made that deal in 1995, despite the fact that Coca-Cola was the NFL's official soft drink—it had paid the NFL to be the only beverage able to call itself that.

Occasionally, these types of exclusive agreements get even more complicated. When superstar basketball player and Pepsi pitchman Shaquille O'Neal joined the Los Angeles Lakers, Coca-Cola backed out of a sponsorship deal it had with the Lakers. "It makes no sense for Coca-Cola to sponsor a team whose marquee player endorses the competition," said a Coca-Cola spokesman. "Sports is huge business now. The stakes have been raised pretty high because of all the money that's involved. And companies have to protect their own interests."

Proposals for new sports facilities and remodeling of existing buildings

Dallas Cowboys owner Jerry Jones

SPORTS AND COMMERCIALISM

The price fans pay for their tickets is only a fraction of what most spend for a few hours at the ballpark. More and more, owners try to get a share of the other money—for parking, refreshments, and souvenirs.

always include luxury suites that corporations or fans with deep pockets can lease for events. These private rooms overlooking the action vary in size and usually contain private restrooms and include a selection of food and beverages. If fans have difficulty seeing all the action below, they can turn to a close-up view shown on a closed-circuit television monitor nearby. In 1996, prices for luxury suites in NBA arenas ranged from $50,000 to $200,000 a year. Playing in their new arena, the United Center, the Chicago Bulls reportedly generated $24 million from more than 200 luxury suites.

Companies also shell out big bucks to have their signs shown in

A BIG TICKET

stadiums and on scoreboards during events. Often, these signs are visible during television coverage of the game, increasing their value to advertisers. For the team owners, the signs are another way to increase profits. Unlike many league-wide licensing arrangements, these funds go directly to the team and aren't shared with other owners.

The most expensive sign of all is the one that hangs outside the building. More and more new sports facilities are being named for corporations that pay millions of dollars for the privilege. The Bulls' United Center is named for United Airlines. The Milwaukee Brewers reached an agreement with Miller Brewing Company to call the team's new ballpark Miller Park. Newspapers reported the deal will cost Miller $41 million over 23 years. The going rate in the late 1990s was $30 million to $50 million for 10 to 30 years. After a contract runs out, a team is free to sell naming rights for the facility to someone else. In many cases, fees for naming rights are factored into stadium financing proposals.

In the face of high player salaries and huge franchise fees, new owners insist they need all the revenues they can generate from stadiums to keep their team finances healthy.

Source: Deady, Tim. "Shaq's Soft Drink Sponsorship Demonstrates Clout of Athletes." *Los Angeles Business Journal,* 9 September 1996.

Advertising is everywhere in sports.

SPORTS AND COMMERCIALISM

angers many. "I think a question that has to be asked is, in a time of poverty and homelessness and crime and all the other problems this society has, should we be building $400 million stadiums with public funds," said Roone Arledge. "In most cases, these stadiums are publicly financed but privately profitable. And there are very few other places where that is true."[2]

In 1985, St. Louis Cardinals football team owner William Bidwill asked for a $170 million domed stadium. The city, desperate to keep the team, offered to build a $117 million outdoor stadium, but Bidwill refused. He held out for offers from other cities, and as talks dragged on for more than three years, other cities offered more money and incentives. St. Louis sweetened its offer, including a $5 million practice facility and office complex, low rent at Busch Stadium, and a new domed stadium with 65 luxury skyboxes.

In the end, St. Louis couldn't beat Phoenix's offer. The Cardinals would play in Arizona State University stadium, and revenues from skyboxes and high-priced seats would go to Bidwill. Arizonans paid a $10 million franchise fee, promised a $5 million practice facility, and agreed to split money from concessions and parking with Bidwill.

A similar scenario developed in 1995, when Cleveland Browns owner Art Modell announced plans to move his football team to Baltimore. While Baltimore residents were thrilled to have an NFL team back in town—the Baltimore Colts had fled the city for

Despite a large and loyal following for the Browns, owner Art Modell moved the team from Cleveland.

A BIG TICKET

Cleveland fans turned out at a winter NFL business meeting hopeful of persuading NFL owners to block the Browns' move.

Indianapolis in the middle of the night years earlier—the loyal Cleveland fans were outraged. The city tried to make Modell honor his lease at Cleveland Stadium. Groups of fans filed lawsuits. Advertisers and sponsors canceled their business deals with the team. Fans and city leaders lobbied NFL owners to vote against Modell's move.

Early in 1996, it was clear the team would be allowed to move. But Cleveland fans had earned a

SPORTS AND COMMERCIALISM

major concession: Modell would not be able to take the name Browns with him. Instead, his team would become the Baltimore Ravens, and Cleveland would retain the Browns name for a new team the NFL promised to bring the city in 1999.

By the time Modell moved his team to Baltimore, the NFL had returned to St. Louis when the Rams moved there from the Los Angeles area. Raiders owner Al Davis had already moved his team back to Oakland, so for the first time in half a century

The team formerly known as the Cleveland Browns became the Baltimore Ravens after relocating. The NFL promised a new Cleveland Browns team by 1999.

THE PACKERS: REALLY GREEN BAY'S TEAM

Unlike other sports fans, residents of Green Bay, Wisconsin, never have to worry about their football team moving to another city. The Green Bay Packers have a unique system of ownership: community members own the team. The team charter prevents the Packers from ever leaving Green Bay.

The Packers are owned by about 1,900 shareholders. Each shareholder owns one or more shares, or equal portions, of the business. Each share is valued at just $25. Owners can't sell their shares; they can only give them to relatives or return them to the Packers.

With all these owners, who runs the team? Shareholders elect a board of directors, which hires management to run the football team. When the Packers make a profit, shareholders don't get any money. Instead, the profits are used to operate the team and to improve its facilities. In recent years, the team has used its profits to add luxury boxes to the city-owned Lambeau Field and to build an indoor practice facility.

If the Packers *were* sold, according to rules established by the team's founders, profits from the sale would be used to build a war memorial at an American Legion post in Green Bay. It would be quite a memorial, since NFL teams cost $150 million in the mid-1990s, although no one expects the team ever to be sold.

Unless the NFL changes its rules, no other team will be operated the same way. Green Bay first became a nonprofit entity in 1922, and the current ownership arrangement was established in 1946. It was only much later that the NFL enacted a rule specifying that teams must have one person who has authority to make team decisions and owns at least 30 percent of the team. Because the Packers' system existed before the rule, Green Bay is allowed to keep its community ownership through a grandfather clause—an exemption from the rule.

The Packers are clearly winners with Wisconsin fans, regardless of the team's won-lost record. Season tickets have been sold out for years, and the waiting list to purchase those few tickets that become available each year has tens of thousands of names.

SPORTS AND COMMERCIALISM   51

A BIG TICKET

there was no NFL team for Los Angeles fans. Distressed because one of the country's largest TV markets had no pro football team, commissioner Paul Tagliabue vowed the NFL would return to Los Angeles.

IT TAKES MONEY TO MAKE MONEY

Most professional teams are owned by diverse groups, ranging from private individuals to large corporations. Teams don't come cheap. When the Baltimore Orioles changed owners in 1989, the price tag was $70 million. The Orioles were sold again in 1993—for $173 million.

For owners of a new team, startup costs include a franchise fee, the cost of joining a league. That fee is divided among the rest of the owners in the league. Franchise fees have climbed as dramatically as players' salaries in recent years. The cost of joining

The cost of buying a sports franchise may lead to more corporate ownership arrangements. The Mighty Ducks—the NHL team and the fictional team featured in movies—are owned by Disney.

the NFL in 1920 was $100. In 1976, the cost was $16 million. In 1991, the price rose to $150 million. In baseball, the franchise fee was $7 million in 1977. In 1990, it was $95 million. The NBA charged new owners $12 million in 1980. By 1989, that figure had jumped to $32 million, and by 1995, it was $125 million.

At such prices, professional teams might soon be out of reach of individual owners. Increasingly, owners are corporations—such as Disney, which owns the Mighty Ducks and the Angels.

A photograph of Michael Jordan greeted commuters during the Barcelona Olympics.

CHAPTER FOUR

SELLING STARS

Sprinters Tommie Smith and John Carlos risked their lives and careers when they raised their fists in protest on the medal stand at the 1968 Olympic Games in Mexico City. Their symbolic, powerful gesture, which they choreographed minutes after finishing the 200-meter race, was meant to awaken the world to racial injustice in the United States. They paid the price for their action: Smith and Carlos were banished from the Olympic Village and shunned by employers at home.

In 1992, Michael Jordan and some other members of the hailed U.S. basketball team also protested on the medal stand at the Olympics. As the so-called Dream Team gathered to receive their gold medals, some members draped American flags over their shoulders.

Was this a demonstration of patriotism? Not exactly. The players were using the flags to cover up the Reebok logo on their warm-up suits. Jordan, Charles Barkley, David Robinson, Scottie Pippen, John Stockton, and Chris Mullin had deals to endorse Nike products. But Reebok was an official sponsor of the U.S. Olympic

A BIG TICKET

In a flap about loyalty to sponsors, the players on the 1992 Dream Team hid the Reebok logo on their warm-up jackets.

team. The Olympic committee ruled that the players had to wear the Reebok suits if they wanted to get a medal.

The Dream Team's stand shows how loyalty to a company has become as important as allegiance to country and team. Winning isn't the only thing anymore. What shoes a player wears, how big his smile is, and what cola he drinks are just as important. To advertisers, an athlete's popularity might be more valuable than his jump shot.

Sports is entertainment, and athletes are its stars. Good looks and personality can land athletes an endorsement contract—a deal to appear in advertisements or to

SPORTS AND COMMERCIALISM

serve as a company's spokesperson. Rare is the NBA player without the Nike swoosh on his shoes or the tennis player without a company logo on his or her sleeve.

The sponsors and the sponsored have a give-and-take relationship. Athletes who advertise or display a company's products help boost its public image. In return, sponsors give athletes anything from free clothing and equipment to millions of dollars. Companies sometimes sponsor whole teams or governing organizations; in the 1990s, Campbell Soup Company sponsored the U.S. Figure Skating Association. In exchange, figure skaters appeared

Sponsorship deals exist in most sports. Should athletes limit the number of sponsorships they accept?

in the company's advertisements.

Having the right athlete promote a product is worth far more than the price of a commercial. When a player wins a major tennis tournament, highlights of the winning match no doubt will be shown on the evening news. Television viewers across the country will see that player—and the company logo on his or her sleeve—even if they didn't watch the actual match. For the company, the price of sponsoring the athlete is small compared to the widespread exposure and image-boosting it gets in return.

NIKE'S IMPACT

The relationship between advertisers and athletes blossomed in the 1980s when a Chicago Bulls basketball player and a Oregon-based shoe company joined forces. Together, Michael Jordan and Nike redefined fame and lifted each other to new heights. Like no other athlete, Jordan inspired consumers to buy Nike products—specifically, colorful basketball shoes bearing his name, Air Jordan.

In innovative ads directed by filmmaker Spike Lee, Jordan became one of the most recognized people in the world and the most sought-after corporate spokesperson. "Nike has done such a job of promoting me that I've turned into a dream," Jordan said. "In some ways it's taken me away from the game and turned me into an entertainer. To a lot of people I'm just a person who stars in commercials."[1] In 1994, the year in which Jordan played minor-league baseball after briefly retiring from basketball, he earned $30 million from endorse-

Nike has positioned its logo throughout the sports world.

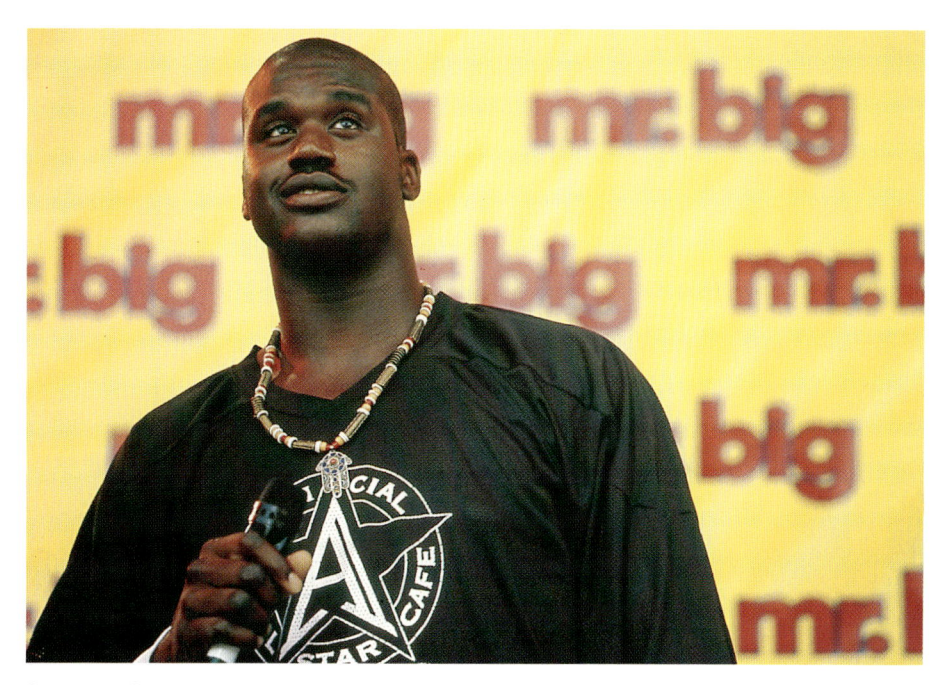

Shaquille O'Neal's ascent as superstar endorser was even faster than Michael Jordan's.

ment deals with Nike and other companies.

Thanks to savvy marketing and Jordan's widespread popularity, Nike saw unbounded growth. Its presence in sports goes far and deep. By 1993, more than 80 percent of NBA players wore Nikes, and more than 60 big-time colleges had agreed to outfit their players in Nikes. The numbers are just as high in the NFL and Major League Baseball.

But Nike's influence spreads beyond sports. The company secured a prominent place in mainstream culture as athletic shoes became a fashion standard on the streets of the United States and throughout the world.

Nike's successful formula inspired Reebok and other rivals to sign promising rookies, such as Shaquille O'Neal, to endorsement deals. Endorsements have become so important that during the NBA draft, there is almost as much talk about which shoe company an athlete will represent as which team will draft him.

THE RIGHT FORMULA

Few endorsers have the staying power of golfer Arnold Palmer, who in 1994 earned $13.5 million from endorsements, even though he hadn't won a PGA tournament in more than 20 years. What makes athletes such as Jordan and Palmer more desirable than others? There is no certain formula. Often, success depends on a combination of timing, looks, personality, and athletic ability.

Arnold Palmer continued to attract endorsement deals long after his income from golf titles diminished.

Are the Jensen brothers good for tennis?

Charisma is key. Brothers Luke and Murphy Jensen aren't top seeds in tennis. The doubles duo doesn't win much—they often don't last past the opening rounds. But almost as many teens recognize the Jensens as recognize top-rated players Michael Chang and Boris Becker. With their grunge-rock image and antics on the court, they've made "tennis cool again," said Luke Jensen. For the Jensens, image, entertainment, and marketing are just as important as winning. "Letting your racket speak for itself doesn't sell the game,"[2] says Luke. The brothers boast one of the longest list of sponsors in tennis, and promoters pay them up to $20,000 just for showing up at tournaments.

Despite their popularity, the contribution the Jensens have

A BIG TICKET

made to tennis is arguable. Critics say the Jensen brothers are all show, and that their success demonstrates how style has become more important than athletic ability in professional sports. But supporters say the Jensens have brought life to a sport that often has a reputation for stuffiness.

Though corporations may embrace crowd pleasers such as the Jensens, they shy away from controversy. Basketball player Magic Johnson of the Los Angeles Lakers saw his appeal as an endorser drop after he announced he had tested positive for HIV, the virus that causes AIDS. Many speculate that Martina Navratilova, one of the best tennis players of all time, makes considerably less endorsement money than her counterparts because she is openly homosexual. In 1992, Navratilova earned $2 million from endorsements, while Steffi Graf, who had won fewer Grand Slam tournaments, earned three times more.

For advertisers, reputation is a big part of the equation. Take the example of hockey player Wayne Gretzky. In corporate and mainstream America's eyes, Gretzky has what it takes. Beginning his career in Canada, he established

Despite her numerous singles titles, Martina Navratilova (top) received far fewer endorsement opportunities than Steffi Graf.

SPORTS AND COMMERCIALISM 63

Hockey superstar Wayne Gretzky made far more money from endorsements after the Edmonton Oilers sent him to Los Angeles.

himself as "the Great One." He has led teams to hockey's highest honor, the Stanley Cup, four times and has broken nearly every league record. But, just as important, he projects an image of a clean-cut, polite family man who treats fans, reporters, teammates, and friends with respect. What advertiser wouldn't want him hawking its products?

Though Gretzky established his dominance on the ice in Canada, his financial fortunes didn't change dramatically until he was traded to the Los Angeles Kings. In a city that thrives on celebrity, Gretzky became a rich man. Teaming up with companies eager to profit from his name, he created an empire of endorsements. His name is linked with everything from hockey sticks and in-line skates to restaurants, soft drinks, pizza, and consumer electronics. In 1994, he padded his

$11.6 million per season salary from the Los Angeles Kings with approximately $23.5 million in endorsement money.

Corporations have a lot to gain by linking their names to rising stars. But in the quest for the next Michael Jordan, advertisers have been known to jump the gun. One of the most famous failures was Reebok's much-hyped "Dan and Dave" commercial spots. The ads featured U.S. decathletes Dan O'Brien and Dave Johnson and played up their rivalry, which was to be settled at the Olympic Games in Barcelona in 1992.

The ad campaign came to a crashing halt when O'Brien, a medal favorite, failed to qualify for the Olympic team. The failure of the Reebok campaign shows how shaky sponsorship can be. Circumstances such as injuries, retirement, and controversy can throw a wrench in advertisers' multimillion-dollar plans.

BASEBALL'S IMAGE PROBLEM

Baseball has huge appeal in the memorabilia industry. Fortunes have been built around trading cards, player autographs, and merchandise bearing team logos. But advertisers have yet to find a baseball player with as much charisma as Michael Jordan. "National advertisers haven't been in love with baseball players for a long time,"[3] said Nova Lanktree, president of a Chicago sports marketing company. In the 1990s, only a handful of baseball players had landed deals to appear in national advertisements.

Baseball stars such as Cal Ripken Jr. have qualities advertisers usually love. Ripken, the Baltimore Orioles shortstop, is a down-to-earth family man, clean-cut, and enormously popular with fans. He became more famous after breaking Lou Gehrig's American record of playing in 2,130 straight games. With standout players such as Ripken, why can't baseball and advertisers make the relationship work? The answer lies, in part, in the way games are played and shown.

Baseball players work in pants and often long sleeves, spread out on large playing fields. Action is uneven, with long stretches of time between pitches and hits. By contrast, in basketball, 10 muscular men wearing shorts and sleeveless shirts battle on a small court. On TV, the action is up close and fast, and even a novice

COLLECTING CARDS: HOBBY OR INVESTMENT?

Trading cards—small cards that feature players' pictures and statistics—are a baseball tradition. The first cards were made in 1887 and distributed inside cigarette packs. Bubble gum companies followed suit. By the 1950s, the popularity of the cards had soared. Children and adults alike collected and traded the cards, which were sold with gum for 1 to 5 cents a pack.

Topps chewing gum company became the biggest name in the trading card industry. The company signed contracts with most major and minor league players for the exclusive right to use their photos. At first, Topps paid players a flat fee each year. Later, players negotiated for a share of the profits.

Trading cards are produced for other sports, such as football, basketball, and hockey. But sales of these cards aren't as high as those of baseball cards. Sales of baseball trading cards were about $1.3 billion in 1991.

Not only do the companies that produce the cards make money but so do collectors. The value of a trading card can increase dramatically over time. A 1953 Mickey Mantle card from Topps sold for $100 in the late 1970s and was worth about $1,400 by the mid-1990s. The first Mantle card from Topps was valued at $25,000 in 1996. In recent years, however, manufacturers have produced so many cards that newer cards seldom hold more than their original value.

---

viewer can quickly recognize faces and understand the game. Players' personalities shine in basketball like no other sport. Spectators can see their expressions, grace, and physical power.

"The personalities of people like Michael Jordan and Charles Barkley far exceed those of any baseball players," said advertising executive Nick Gisondi. "There are no Reggie Jacksons out there.

Who's the biggest personality in baseball today? [Yankees owner] George Steinbrenner?"[4] Some baseball players have attracted major endorsement deals, namely Deion Sanders and Bo Jackson. But their appeal was largely based on their dual talents in football and baseball.

The difference might also lie in the shoes. Sporting gear companies such as Nike and Reebok don't run national ads for baseball spikes because few people wear them. Baseball wear has little street appeal. Basketball shoes, on the other hand, can be worn everyday by anyone. The shoes are big sellers, accounting for the largest piece of a $7.5 billion sports shoe market. Wholesale sales of basketball shoes reached about $1.6 billion in 1990. Most were made by the big players: Nike, Reebok, Converse, L.A. Gear, and Adidas.

A CHANGING LANDSCAPE

Athletes aren't the only ones promoting products. Ads are everywhere within sports stadiums: on the walls, on the game clock, on the cups from which players drink. Even the once-empty spot behind home plate at Yankee Stadium is available for advertising to anyone who will pay $100,000. A 1992 Ernst & Young study showed that for the 105 professional teams in 44 cities in North America, more than 4,400 signs in stadiums touted the products of about 1,400 advertisers.

With many games on television, the signage reaches an even bigger audience. And television viewers are bombarded more heavily with corporate messages than their counterparts in stadiums. Never mind traditional commercials. Even halftime reports and instant replays bear the names of corporate sponsors.

More and more, new stadiums and arenas are named for corporate backers. Advertisers commonly pay to have their names added to events such as college football bowl games. The new roll call is a mouthful. The Gator Bowl became the Outback Steakhouse Gator Bowl. The Alamo Bowl turned into the Builders Square Alamo Bowl.

Most golf and tennis tournaments also take the name of their sponsors. And every time an announcer or sportswriter refers to the event by its full name, the company gets publicity that's often cheaper and more effective than advertising time purchased on television.

In 1993, Coors Brewing Company introduced a new minor league baseball team, the all-female Silver Bullets, named after Coors's Silver Bullet beer. The team is not the first sports group to be named after a product—and it won't be the last. The Anaheim Mighty Ducks hockey team is named after a team from a movie.

The Silver Bullets baseball team was named after a beer.

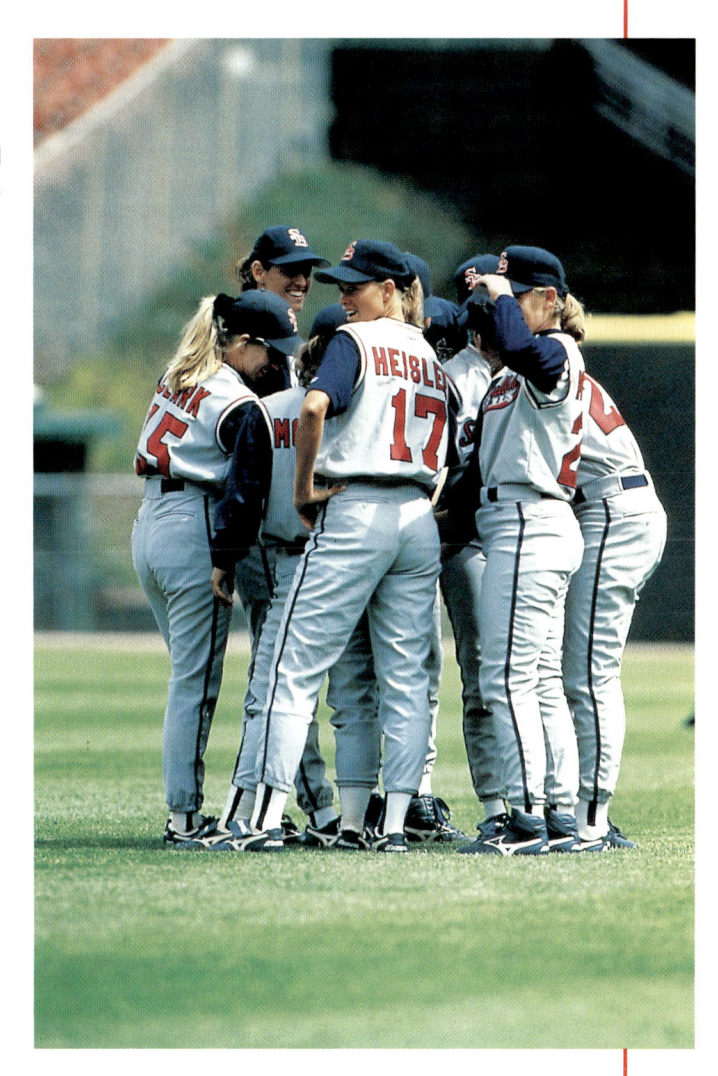

SHOES TO DIE FOR

For many teens, a pair of Air Jordans or a professional team jacket brings status. Fifteen-year-old Michael Thomas was a big Michael Jordan fan. The ninth grader's prize possession was a $115 pair of Nike's Air Jordan shoes.

In the spring of 1989, Thomas was killed by another youth who wanted his expensive sneakers. He was one of at least seven youths killed for their athletic shoes between 1985 and 1989.

The violence sparked accusations that Nike markets its products to poor, black youths in the inner cities. A Nike public relations director countered: "We don't target a market to a demographic [specific group]. . . . We sell to passions and states of mind, not by age, address, or ethnicity." Although Nike refused to take blame for the violence, an outraged public criticized Nike for helping to create a culture in which owning a pair of shoes is so important that people are willing to murder for them.

Source: Katz, Donald. "Triumph of the Swoosh." *Sports Illustrated,* 16 August 1993, p. 71.

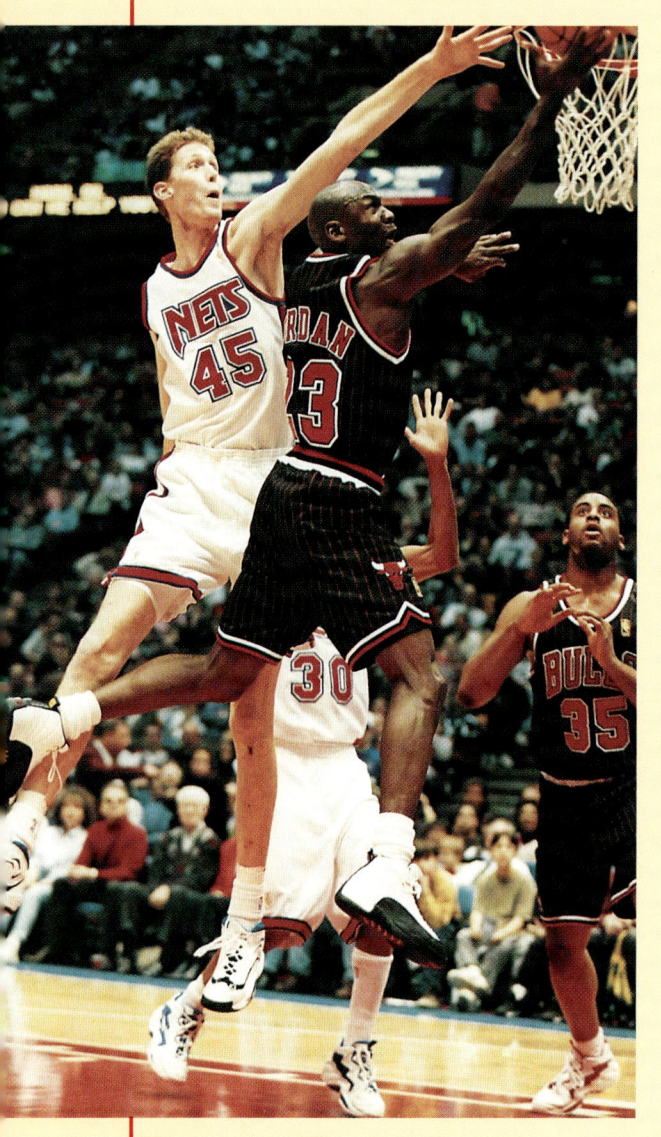

Have basketball players and footwear companies made shoes too popular?

Sports-related clothing is a burgeoning industry.

SPORTS FASHION

Walk into any mall in the United States and you'll see Raiders jackets, Broncos hats, and Bulls jerseys. "This type of apparel has suddenly become very fashionable. I eat dinner in a restaurant, and I see people wearing Dallas Cowboy sweaters. That's how they want to dress today,"[5] said Dan McElwain, marketing programs manager at J.C. Penney.

The new Colorado Rockies baseball team sold more black-and-purple Rockies products in 1992 than two long-established teams, the Mets and Dodgers—before even playing a single game. Before two new NBA teams, the

A BIG TICKET

New sports franchises get the merchandising wheels for logo-driven products turning before the team even has its first player.

Toronto Raptors and the Vancouver Grizzlies, chose players, they sold millions of dollars in merchandise.

Each league sells merchandising rights, which allow manufacturers to create specific products—jackets, balls, shirts, shorts, and caps—decorated with team logos. For example, the National Football League determines which clothing company can make Broncos T-shirts, Raiders hats, and so forth and licenses—sells formal permission to—companies to produce the merchandise. Though one team's products might sell more than another's, all teams divide the profits equally.

In 1985, sales for licensed NFL products were $5.5 billion. That figure grew to $12.2 billion in 1992. In Major League Baseball, merchandise sales were more than $2.3 billion in 1992. In 1995, the NBA estimated sales of licensed products would generate nearly $3 billion worldwide.

72　A BIG TICKET

If he had competed in the late part of the 20th century, Jesse Owens's financial situation would have been much better.

CHAPTER FIVE

AMATEURS NO MORE

On playing fields and in recreation centers across the United States, people run, bowl, swim, and play softball, golf, and tennis for reasons that have little to do with money. Little leagues, junior soccer leagues, and high school sports are amateur pursuits.

In amateur sports, athletes aren't paid to compete. But in recent years, television, endorsement deals, and big businesses have encroached on amateur athletics. Where there were once strict lines between the amateur and pro ranks, definitions have begun to blur.

THE CHANGING OLYMPICS

For nearly 100 years, athletes who received money for their skills were barred from competing in the Olympic Games. The founder of the modern Olympics, French Baron Pierre de Coubertin, envisioned a contest for amateurs only and strongly fought to keep professionals out of the Games.

"An amateur does not rely on sports for his livelihood," remarked Avery Brundage, president of the International Olympic Committee from 1952 to 1972.

"The devotion of the true amateur athlete is the same devotion that makes an artist starve in his garret rather than commercialize his work."[1]

Until the 1980s, most countries sent their best amateurs to the Olympics. For instance, the U.S. Olympic hockey team was made up of top college players. Though most Olympic hopefuls—particularly in individual sports—received a little support from donations, sponsors, and national sports associations, they mostly financed their coaching, travel, and equipment needs by holding part-time jobs.

Athletes from Eastern European and Soviet countries, on the other hand, were sponsored by their governments. Though technically amateurs, these athletes did not need to hold jobs and could devote all of their time to training. They dominated the medal stands, while athletes from other nations lagged in Olympic competition.

Because of this inequity, the idea of amateurism was removed from the Olympic charter in 1981. "What we want is the world's best athletes competing in the Olympic Games. . . . Professional or amateur—we want the best," said Richard Pound, a member of the IOC.[2]

In a sense, the Games are still amateur contests—winners don't receive any prize money from the International Olympic Committee. But, by the 1990s, people who normally got paid for their athletic skills—professional basketball players, for instance—could compete in most events. Individual athletic associations, on a sport-by-sport basis, set the rules on whether professionals can compete.

Professional skater Brian Boitano hoped to compete in the 1992 Olympics when the rules were relaxed.

As an amateur in 1988, Boitano won a gold medal.

Some associations have been slow to open the doors to professionals. Figure skater Brian Boitano wanted to compete in the 1992 Games in Albertville, France. Two years earlier, the International Skating Union had ruled that professionals could compete in the Games—but not if they had participated in non-ISU competitions. Boitano had competed in such an event, the NutraSweet World Professional Figure Skating Championships. He was barred from Olympic competition.

"What gets me is there are other professionals competing at the 1992 Olympic Games when I'm ineligible," Boitano said. "I mean, what's the difference between my competing in skating and Michael Jordan's competing in basketball? There are hockey players being taken off NHL teams. And tennis. Do you remember in Seoul, who won the gold medal in women's tennis? Steffi Graf. I looked at that and I thought, My god, figure skating's going to open up too."[3] Eventually, skating did open up. Boitano competed at the 1994 Winter Games in Lillehammer, Norway, where he finished sixth.

PAYING THE BILLS

The majority of Olympic athletes are not rich, famous professionals. Many are high school and college students who struggle to balance the demands of homework, part-time employment, and training. Some parents drain their bank accounts in hope that their child will peak athletically during an Olympic year. "Parents can spend $30,000 annually on [figure skating] training for years, and that's with no guarantees [of winning]. Ice time alone can run up to $200 a day,"[4] says Brian Boitano.

The U.S. Olympic Committee provides some money to American athletes. Its budget comes from broadcasting fees and donations, mostly from corporate America. The USOC then channels money to national governing bodies, which pay for coaching, training facilities, and travel expenses for each Olympic team.

Few governing bodies are managed as well as USA Volleyball. With a budget of about $3 million, bolstered by money from corporate sponsors, the USAV gives Olympic athletes enough money to train—and even to live comfortably. In 1988, female volleyball players received stipends of $30,000 per year.

In high-profile sports such as figure skating and gymnastics, top Olympic athletes might also land endorsement contracts. Skater Nancy Kerrigan once worked as a waitress and a sales clerk to help finance her training, which cost about $50,000 a year. Eventually, as her success grew, she was able to line up corporate sponsorships. "The lines are blurred between amateur and professional, and I think skating is moving in the direction of breaking down all the barriers," said Kerrigan's agent and husband Jerry Solomon. "Taking money or doing endorsements is not inherently bad."[5]

According to *Sports Illustrated*, 41 percent of the 1996 U.S. Olympic team had endorsement contracts. Many of these athletes, such as the male basketball players, were already famous professionals. But those who compete in less popular Olympic sports such

SPORTS AND COMMERCIALISM 77

Nancy Kerrigan's finances changed as she became more popular and more successful.

A BIG TICKET

as field hockey, shot put, and archery aren't very likely to land endorsement contracts. These athletes have little hope of reaping gold beyond their medals. Few would question their true amateur status.

CASH AND COLLEGE SPORTS

In theory, college sports are also amateur sports. In reality, some college sports are big business. Millions of dollars—from television contracts, ticket sales, and merchandising deals—fund Division I athletic departments and scholarships. In 1990, for instance, Notre Dame sold the rights to broadcast its home football games from 1991 to 1995 for $38 million.

Winning translates into money—from fans, alumni, and television. But the rewards of victory put pressure on colleges to win at any cost. "Because of the huge sums colleges stand to make from television contracts," says Robert

Colleges such as Notre Dame are employing many of the same business strategies as professional leagues do to bring in money.

GAMES TO REVITALIZE A CITY

Atlanta put on its best face for the Olympics.

Hosting the Olympic Games can help a city by bringing in jobs, new buildings, and tourists. Residents of Atlanta, Georgia, hosts of the 1996 Summer Olympics, spent more than nine years trying to land the Games and preparing for the three-week event. Many residents hoped that income from the Games would help revitalize the city's run-down, largely African American neighborhoods.

The most difficult task for the Atlanta Committee for the Olympic Games (ACOG) was raising the $1.6 billion it needed to stage the Games. But city leaders saw the cost as a chance to attract new industry: "A significant percentage of the business leaders and decision makers in the Western World . . . are going to be here. To have the opportunity to impress them . . . it's an opportunity that money couldn't buy," said Billy Payne, ACOG president.

Source: Eddings, Jerelyn. "Atlanta Goes for Olympic Gold." *U.S. News & World Report,* 7 August 1995, p. 28.

80 A BIG TICKET

Do high expectations for successful—and profitable—programs force college coaches to break the rules imposed by the NCAA?

Lipsyte, columnist for *The New York Times,* "many schools have virtually mortgaged themselves to their sports programs."

To keep their teams successful, coaches desperately try to recruit promising high school players. Sometimes, in direct violation of NCAA rules, coaches lure players with gifts and money. "Colleges have no choice but to compete among themselves for athletes who will draw crowds to those stadiums," continues Lipsyte, "and that has corrupted the recruiting system."[6]

Student-athletes who help their teams win are often treated like celebrities, much like their professional counterparts. But, unlike

Should star college athletes be allowed to share the money they help generate for their schools? Are NCAA rules about athletes and money too harsh?

SCHOOL CLOTHES

Money from ticket sales has always been the primary source of income for Division I college athletic departments. But schools can only raise ticket prices so far without alienating fans and athletes' families. The top college teams benefit from television contracts. But only 10 to 20 NCAA athletic programs consistently make profits. The rest break even or lose money.

To find another way to make money from sports, universities have followed the course of their professional brethren, cashing in on the demand for sports merchandise. At first, schools tried to stay out of the commercial fray. But as the NBA and NFL beefed up their bank accounts with merchandising money, and television made the names and uniforms of college teams famous, schools couldn't ignore the commercial potential any longer. In 1994, sales of merchandise bearing college team logos reached about $2.5 billion—$100 million of which went to schools because of licensing agreements.

The University of Michigan is one of academia's leaders in merchandising. The school's success is attributed to its teams' winning streaks, national exposure, a large alumni base, and the fame of the Fab Five—five players whose skills on the basketball court in the early 1990s and penchant for baggy shorts inspired teenagers to shell out cash so they could look the same way.

Merchandising money gives Michigan some shelter from budget cuts. "The licensing thing has really been an unexpected windfall for us," said Bob DeCarolis, associate athletic director for business. "We've dodged the bullet."

Source: Rubin, Dana. "You've Seen the Game, Now Buy the Underwear." *The New York Times,* 11 September 1994, Sec. 3, p. 5.

SPORTS AND COMMERCIALISM 83

professionals, students don't see a share of the money they help bring into universities. Many athletes attend school on scholarships. NCAA regulations forbid them to hold jobs on the side. Payments to student-athletes—from coaches, alumni, or anyone else—are violations of NCAA rules.

In such an environment, agents can easily tempt student-athletes, whose financial dreams hinge on landing a lucrative pro contract. In 1994, at least seven players on the Florida State University football team were accused of accepting cash payments from agents. At one point, agents took players to a Foot Locker store and paid for a $6,000 shopping spree. The illegal gifts and payments resulted in embarrassment at Florida State, the suspension of four football players, and the conviction of agents.

Athletes can receive scholarships that pay for their education and room and board, but NCAA rules prevent them from holding jobs to earn spending money.

SPORTS AND COMMERCIALISM

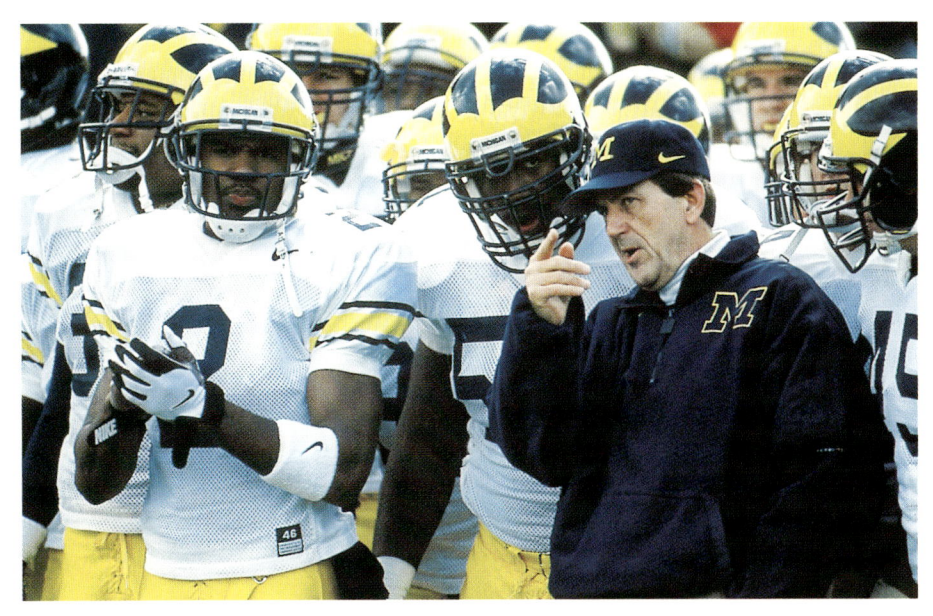

Coaches often get paid nicely to have their teams wear a certain manufacturer's uniform—and display its logo. The athletes can't receive any money for helping to promote the manufacturer.

Critics say that such corruption stems from the myth that college sports are amateur sports. Sure, the student-athletes don't get paid aside from their scholarship money. But, in other respects, Division I college teams are run—and generate money—exactly like professional clubs. "Colleges and universities have become farm clubs for professional basketball and football teams," says sociologist Harry Edwards. "These kids do not come to college looking for an education."[7] Some argue that paying student-athletes—just as journalists on student newspapers sometimes get paid—would help eliminate the hypocrisy and corruption in college sports.

HIGHER, FASTER, RICHER

From college to the Olympics to the professional leagues, commercialism has an undeniable role in the way Americans play and view sports. Money has brought change. In some ways, the change has been negative.

A BIG TICKET

Sponsorships can help brand new or less popular sports get off the ground and attract attention in a crowded sports world.

"Everyone is more interested in money in most cases than they are in sport. And a lot of fun has gone out of it," says Roone Arledge. "The original motivation a lot of us had for wanting to be a part of sports—that no longer exists."[8]

But there are positives, too. Formerly obscure sports have blossomed in the commercial spotlight. Look at figure skating. In 1964, *Wide World of Sports* showed Peggy Fleming winning the National Figure Skating Championships "in a virtually empty arena in Cleveland," said Dennis Lewin, senior vice president of ABC Sports. "Figure skating eventually flourished because of exposure by ABC. Now, you can't buy a ticket to see skating."[9]

Television helps glorify sports and attracts fans. Onscreen graphics, play-by-play announcing, and cameras covering every inch of the field make games such as football more interesting to watch and easier to understand. Sponsors and merchandisers supply badly needed funds to promising athletes and college sports programs.

With or without that big money, though, athletes will still keep pushing their limits. Records will still be broken. Sports will still be exciting. Sometimes the commercial marketplace hurts the game. Sometimes it enhances it. But, whether we like it or not, commercialism in sports is here to stay.

NOTES

CHAPTER ONE: A FRONT-ROW SEAT

1. Rushin, Steve. "1954–1994: How We Got Here." *Sports Illustrated*, 16 August 1994, p. 36.

2. Rushin, "How We Got Here," p. 39.

3. Gorman, Jerry and Kirk Calhoun. *The Name of the Game*. New York: John Wiley & Sons, Inc., 1994, p. 69.

CHAPTER TWO: DOLLAR SIGNS

1. Rushin, "How We Got Here," p. 60.

2. Rushin, "How We Got Here," p. 42.

3. "Scorecard: Wake of the Flood." *Sports Illustrated*, 27 January 1997, p. 19.

4. Swann, Lynn. "In the NFL, a New Set Of Beliefs Suddenly Holds Sway." *The New York Times*, 18 April 1993, Sec. 8, p. 9.

5. Freeman, Mike. "Simms Fades Back and Throws Barbs at Tagliabue." *The New York Times*, 23 July 1994, p. 29.

6. King, Peter. "Show Of Arms," *Sports Illustrated*, 25 April 1994, p. 28.

7. Swift, E. M., "From Corned Beef to Caviar." *Sports Illustrated*, 3 June 1991, pp. 82–83.

8. King, Peter. "Money Can't Buy Success." *Sports Illustrated*, 31 October 1994, p. 20.

9. Powers, John. "Wheelers and Dealers." *The Boston Globe*, 5 July 1987, p. 43.

10. Finn, Robin. "Never Too Young for Tennis Millions." *The New York Times*, 10 November 1993, p. B25.

11. Kinkopf, Eric, and Terry Foster. "Agents: A Question of Trust." *Detroit Free Press*, 7 February 1988, p. H1.

12. Kinkopf and Foster, "Agents."

CHAPTER THREE: GROWTH SPURT

1. Donelly, Harrison. "High Stakes of Sports Economics." *Editorial Research Reports*, 8 April 1988, p. 174

2. Rushin, "How We Got Here," p. 42.

CHAPTER FOUR: SELLING STARS

1. Katz, Donald. "Triumph of the Swoosh." *Sports Illustrated*, 16 August 1993, p. 60.

2. Frank, Robert. "Jensen Brothers May Not Win at Tennis, But Fans and Sponsors Go Wild for Them." *The Wall Street Journal,* 17 May 1995, p. B1.

3. Elliott, Stuart. "Marketers Finding Other Games to Play." *The New York Times,* 11 August 1994, p. D2.

4. Sandomir, Richard. "Superstars, But Not In Adland." *The New York Times,* 4 April 1993, Sec. 3, p. 8.

5. Steinbreder, John. "Hot Properties." *Sports Illustrated,* 9 March 1992, p. 5.

CHAPTER FIVE: AMATEURS NO MORE

1. Johnson, William Oscar. "Goodbye Olive Wreaths; Hello, Riches and Reality." *Sports Illustrated,* 9 February 1987, pp. 174–176.

2. Johnson, "Goodbye Olive Wreaths," pp. 176–178.

3. Swift, E. M. "Brian Boitano." *Sports Illustrated,* 10 February 1992, p. 63.

4. Swift, "Brian Boitano."

5. Finn, Robin. "Money Is Music To Their Ears." *The New York Times,* 25 October 1992, Sec. 8, p. 12.

6. Guterson, David. "Moneyball! On the Relentless Promotion of Pro Sports." *Harper's,* September 1994, p. 47.

7. Guterson, "Moneyball!" p. 54.

8. Rushin, "How We Got Here," p. 65.

9. Hoffer, Richard. "Spanning the Globe for 30 Years." *Sports Illustrated,* 27 May 1991, p. 92.

SELECTED BIBLIOGRAPHY

Alexander, Charles P. "A Called Strike Looms." *Time,* 29 July 1985.

Angeli, Michael. "The Gall of Fame." *Sports Illustrated,* 2 August 1993.

Banks, Lacy J. "The Price of Fame." *Sport,* December 1993.

Barbash, Louis. "Clean Up or Pay Up." *Washington Monthly,* July-August 1990.

Basralian, Joseph and Keri Goldman. "Amateurs at Best . . . When It Comes to Making Money, College Athletic Departments Talk a Good Game." *Financial World,* 14 February 1995.

Behar, Richard. "Spreading the Wealth." *Forbes,* 10 August 1987.

Benoit, Ellen, and Colleti, Richard J. "Lost Youth." *Financial World,* 20 September 1988.

Brownlee, Shannon. "The Myth of the Student-Athlete." *U.S. News & World Report,* 8 January 1990.

Chad, Norman. "A Pay-Per-Viewpoint." *Sports Illustrated,* 2 March 1992.

Clay, Bobby. "Black Agents Compete for Blue Chip Athletes." *Black Enterprise,* July 1992.

Cope, Myron. "Would You Let This Man Interview You?" *Sports Illustrated,* 21 March 1994.

Cosell, Howard and Shelby Whitfield. *What's Wrong with Sports.* New York: Simon & Schuster, 1991.

Deacon, James. "Gretzky Inc." *Maclean's,* 5 December 1994.

———. "Road Show." *Maclean's,* 10 April 1995.

Eddings, Jerelyn. "Atlanta Goes for Olympic Gold." *U.S. News & World Report,* 7 August 1995.

Edwards, Harry. "NFL Free Agency and Salary Cap: A Whole New Ball Game." *Sports,* October 1991.

Fennell, Tom and Ann Walmsley. "A Promotional Gamble: Millions Are Riding on Star Athletes." *Maclean's,* 9 April 1990.

Fennell, Tom and D'Arcy Jenish. "The Riches of Sport." *Maclean's,* 9 April 1990.

Finegan, Jay. "Surviving in the Nike/Reebok Jungle." *Inc.,* May 1993.

Forest, Stephanie Anderson. "To Go for the Gold, You Gotta Have Green: How Corporate America is Quietly Helping Olympic Hopefuls." *Business Week,* 17 February 1992.

Frank, Alan Dodds. "Block That Kick." *Forbes,* 4 November 1985.

Gammons, Peter. "Playing Hardball." *Sports Illustrated,* 12 January 1987.

———. "The Best Money Can Buy." *Sports Illustrated,* 14 December 1987.

Gorman, Jerry and Kirk Calhoun. *The Name of the Game.* New York: John Wiley & Sons, Inc., 1994.

Guterson, David. "Moneyball! On the Relentless Promotion of Pro Sports." *Harper's,* September 1994.

Hackney, Holt. "NHL's Big Gamble." *Financial World,* 30 October 1990.

———. "The New Skins Game." *Financial World,* 14 February 1995.

Hanquet, Pierre. "A Bright but Flickering Flame." *UNESCO Courier,* December 1992.

Hoffer, Richard. "Spanning the Globe for 30 Years." *Sports Illustrated,* 27 May 1991.

———. "The Buck Stops Here." *Sports Illustrated,* 29 July 1991.

Jaffe, Harry. "Punch Drunk." *Regardie's Magazine,* September 1990.

Jenkins, Sally. "Billie Jean King." *Sports Illustrated,* 19 September 1994.

———. "The Sorry State of Tennis." *Sports Illustrated,* 9 May 1994.

Johnson, William Oscar. "Goodbye Olive Wreaths; Hello, Riches and Reality." *Sports Illustrated,* 9 February 1987.

———. "The Push Is On: Some Inspired Atlantans Have Propelled Their City to the Verge of Landing the 1996 Olympic Games." *Sports Illustrated,* 27 August 1990.

Kasky, Jillian. "The Best Buys for Fans Today." *Money,* October 1994.

———. "The Best Ticket Buys for Sports Fans Today." *Money,* October 1995.

King, Peter. "Money Can't Buy Success." *Sports Illustrated,* 31 October 1994.

———. "Money Men." *Sports Illustrated,* 12 April 1993.

———. "Perils of a New Era." *Sports Illustrated,* 6 September 1993.

———. "Show of Arms." *Sports Illustrated,* 25 April 1994.

Kirkpatrick, Curry. "For All His Fame and Fortune, Jordan Is, at Heart, Just a Carolina Kid Called Mike." *Sports Illustrated,* 23 December 1991.

———. "Steppin' Out." *Sports Illustrated,* 27 May 1991.

Kirshenbaum, Jerry. "An American Disgrace." *Sports Illustrated,* 27 February 1989.

Klatell, David A. and Norman Marcus. *Sports for Sale.* New York: Oxford University Press, 1988.

Kurkjian, Tim. "Ball of Confusion." *Sports Illustrated,* 9 January 1995.

Kuzela, Lad. "Olympic Boomerang? Business May Pay Too High a Price." *Industry Week,* 6 August 1984.

Lane, Randall. "Prepackaged Celebrity." *Forbes,* 20 December 1993.

———. "The Forbes All-Stars." *Forbes,* 19 December 1994.

Layden, Tim. "Small Change." *Sports Illustrated,* 26 December 1994–2 January 1995.

Levin, Gary. "Baseball's Endorsement Shutout." *Advertising Age,* 15 February 1993.

Levin, Susanna. "The Spoils of Victory: Who Gets Big Money from Sponsors, and Why." *Women's Sports and Fitness,* April 1992.

Lieber, Jill. "Fat and Unhealthy." *Sports Illustrated,* 27 April 1992.

Lipsyte, Robert. "The Dying Game: Why Major League Baseball Has Gotten Too Big for Its Own Jockstrap." *Esquire,* April 1993.

Machan, Dyan, and Vicki Contavespi. "'Compounded Interest' Are Our Favorite Words." *Forbes,* 19 December 1994.

Maisel, Ivan. "Ball Park Figures? Better Believe It." *Sports Illustrated,* 4 March 1985.

McCallum, Jack. "Blame the Bosses." *Sports Illustrated,* 10 October 1994.

———. "USA Inc." *Sports Illustrated,* 22 July 1992.

McGraw, Dan and Richard Bierck. "Playing the Stadium Game." *U.S. News & World Report,* June 3, 1996.

Millman, Joel. "A Piece of the Rocky." *Forbes,* 20 June 1994.

Montville, Leigh. "Forward Progress." *Sports Illustrated,* 5 September 1994.

———. "The First to be Free: In 1976, Baseball's First Free Agents Landed the Big, Big Money." *Sports Illustrated,* 16 April 1990.

Moore, Kenny. "The Spoils of Victory." *Sports Illustrated,* 10 April 1989.

———. "Ties That Bind." *Sports Illustrated,* 27 April 1987.

Morrow, David J. "How to Quit Losing in the Olympics." *Fortune,* 24 April 1989.

Neff, Craig. "A Clean Sweep: How to Deal With Agents." *Sports Illustrated,* 19 October 1987.

Quinn, Hal. "Driving PGA Inc." *Maclean's,* 10 April 1989.

Reed, William F. "All Shook Up: Seismic Shifts Are Altering the Sport's Landscape." *Sports Illustrated,* 26 August 1991.

Reingold, Jennifer. "Thriving on Chaos: Boxing Still Commands Big Bucks, But the Power Is Concentrated in Fewer Hands." *Financial World,* 14 February 1995.

Rowe, Jonathan. "Better Red Than Steinbrenner: Why Fans Should Own Their Teams." *Washington Monthly,* May 1986.

Rozin, Skip. "New Money and Old Games: The Hows and Whys of Salary Escalation." *Sport,* November 1991.

Rushin Steve. "1954–1994: How We Got Here." *Sports Illustrated*, 16 August 1994.

———. "Time Travel on the Tube." *Sports Illustrated*, Special Issue, Fall 1992.

Sanoff, Alvin P. "Baseball Owners Play Tough on Salaries." *U.S. News & World Report*, 13 April 1987.

———. "Not All is Super for Pro Football." *U.S. News & World Report*, 21 January 1985.

Saporito, Bill. "The Owners' New Game is Managing." *Fortune*, 1 July 1991.

Steinbreder, John. "Baskets Full of Money." *Sports Illustrated*, 4 December 1989.

———. "Hot Properties." *Sports Illustrated*, 9 March 1992.

Steptoe, Sonja and E. M. Swift, "Anatomy of a Scandal." *Sports Illustrated*, 16 May 1994.

———. "Child's Play." Sports Illustrated, 10 June 1991.

Swift, E. M., "Brian Boitano." *Sports Illustrated*, 10 February 1992.

———. "From Corned Beef to Caviar." *Sports Illustrated*, 3 June 1991.

———. "The Most Powerful Man in Sports." *Sports Illustrated*, 21 May 1990.

Swift, E. M., and Robert Sullivan. "An Olympian Quagmire." *Sports Illustrated*, 12 September 1988.

Taafe, William. "Get Out Your Checkbook." *Sports Illustrated*, 11 July 1988.

Telander, Rick. "Something Must Be Done." *Sports Illustrated*, 2 October 1989.

Thigpen, David E. "Is Nike Getting Too Big for Its Shoes?" *Time*, 28 April 1993.

Todd, David. "An Earnings Explosion: Wealthy Athletes, More Money." *Maclean's*, 9 April 1990.

Verducci, Tom. "Big Deals." *Sports Illustrated*, 14 June 1993.

———. "Sign of the Times." *Sports Illustrated*, 3 May 1993.

Waldman, Alan. "The Great QB Shuffle." *Sport*, October 1994.

Weisman, Jacob. "Acolytes in the Temple of Nike." *The Nation*, 17 June 1991.

Weiss, Ann E. *Money Games*. New York, New York: Houghton Mifflin Co., 1993.

Wolff, Alexander. "An Honest Wage." *Sports Illustrated*, 30 May 1991.

Worsnop, Richard L. "Free Agency: Pro Sports' Big Challenge." *Editorial Research Reports*, 9 February 1990.

Wulf, Steve. "Out Foxed." *Sports Illustrated*, 3 January 1994.

———. "Where Have All the Big Spenders Gone?" *Sports Illustrated*, 9 December 1985.

Zoglin, Richard. "The Great TV Takeover: Billion-Dollar Feeds and Ever Expanding Coverage Are Reshaping American Sports." *Time*, 26 March 1990.

INDEX

advertising, 8, 16, 18, 20–23, 44, 45–46, 48, 54, 56–59, 64, 66–67
agency groups, 38
agent, 36–39; definition of, 21; selecting, 38, 39
amateur sports, 73–74
Anaheim Mighty Ducks, 52, 53, 67
Arledge, Roone, 10, 11–13, 25–26, 47, 87
athletes' salaries, 23, 28, 34–35
Atlanta Committee for the Olympic Games (ACOG), 79

Baltimore Orioles, 43, 52, 64
Barkley, Charles, 55, 65
Bidwell, William, 47
Boitano, Brian, 74–76
boxing, 14–15
Bradshaw, Terry, 29
broadcasting rights, 7, 8, 17–20, 23, 78, 82; definition of, 21
Brown, Jim, 25
Brundage, Avery, 73

Chicago Bulls, 45, 46
Cleveland Browns, 47–49
college sports, 78–87; funding for, 78, 82
commercials. *See* advertising
concessions revenues, 44
corporate sponsorship. *See* sponsors
Cossell, Howard, 16, 17
Coubertin, Pierre de, 73

Disney, 52, 53
drafting players, 27, 59
Dream Team (men's basketball), 55–56

endorsements, 8, 55–66, 76–78; definition of, 21; personality *vs.* athletic ability in attracting, 61–62
expansion, 41–43

Flood, Curt, 26–27
Florida State University, 84
franchise fees, 52–53
free agency, 26–33; in baseball, 26–28; in basketball, 31–33; courts rule on, 27, 31; in football, 28–31
free agent, definition of, 21

Graf, Steffi, 62, 76
Grantham, Charles, 33
Green Bay Packers, ownership arrangement, 50
Gretzky, Wayne, 62–64

International Olympic Committee (IOC), 7, 73–74
International Skating Union (ISU), 75

Jackson, Bo, 35–36, 66
Jackson, Reggie, 28, 65
Jensen, Luke and Murphy, 61–62
Johnson, Magic, 62
Jones, Jerry, 44
Jordan, Michael, 7, 54, 55, 58–59, 60, 64, 65, 68, 75

Kentucky Derby, 11
Kerrigan, Nancy, 76, 77
King, Billie Jean, 32
Kuhn, Bowie, 27

labor strikes, 34
licensing. *See* merchandising rights
luxury suites, 44–45, 47, 50

Major League Baseball, 8, 26–28, 34, 41, 71
McNally, Dave, 27
merchandising rights, 8, 59, 68, 69–71, 82; definition of, 21
Messersmith, Andy, 27
Michigan, University of, 82–83
minor league baseball, 11
Modell, Art, 47–49

Monday Night Football, 13–17
Moon, Warren, 31
Mourning, Alonzo, 38

National Basketball Association, 8, 31–33, 41, 71
National Collegiate Athletic Association (NCAA), 80–84
National Football League, 8, 28–31, 41, 71
National Hockey League, 8, 41
Navratilova, Martina, 62
NBA Players Association, 33
New York Yankees, 28, 36
NFL Players Association, 39
Nike Sports Management, 38
Nike, 22–23, 55, 57, 58–59, 66; products linked to violence 68

O'Neal, Shaquille, 44
Olympic athletes, funding for, 76–78
Olympic games, 11, 12, 20; Albertville (Winter 1992), 74, 75; Atlanta (Summer 1996), 79; Barcelona (Summer 1992), 54–56, 64; as forum for issues, 55; Lillehammer (Winter 1994), 76; Mexico City (Summer 1968) 55; professionals allowed to compete, 74–76
ownership of pro sports teams, 50, 51–53

Palmer, Arnold, 60
pay–per–view television, 14
player trades, 26
Pound, Richard, 74
Princeton–Columbia baseball game (1939), 9–10
Professional Golfers' Association (PGA), 7, 60

recruiting for college athletics, 81
Reebok, 55–56, 64, 66
reserve system, definition of, 21
revenue sharing, 33

Ripken, Cal Jr., 64
Ross, Bobby, 36
Rozelle, Pete, 17

salaries for athletes. *See* athletes' salaries
salary cap, 28–31, 34 ; definition of, 21
Sanders, Deion, 22, 66
Seles, Monica, 32
Silver Bullets (baseball team), 67
Simms, Phil, 30–31
Soviet Union, 13
sponsors, 23, 55–58, 66–67, 87; definition of, 21
sports clothes and shoes. *See* merchandising rights
stadiums, 43–47
strikes. *See* labor strikes
Super Bowl, 7, 20–23

Tagliabue, Paul, 30–31, 42, 52
television coverage of sports, 9–23, 46, 87; first televised sports event, 9–11; ratings, 20
television rights. *See* broadcasting rights
Toronto Raptors, 70, 71
trades. *See* player trades
trading cards, 65

U.S. Figure Skating Association, 57–58
U.S. Olympic Committee, 76
U.S. Olympic team, 55–56
United Center, 45, 46
USA Volleyball (USAV), 76

Walters, Norby, 38–39
Wide World of Sports, 12–13, 87
Williams, Richard, 37–38
Williams, Venus, 37–38
Women's Tennis Association, 32

96 A BIG TICKET

ACKNOWLEDGMENTS

Photographs are reproduced by permission of: Simon Bruty/Allsport, pp. 2, 45, 79; © Mickey Pfleger/Sports California, pp. 6, 9, 20, 39, 47, 51, 57; SportsChrome East/West/Robert Tringali Jr., pp. 8, 30, 49, 62 (bottom); Archive Photos, pp. 11, 17; Mike Powell/Allsport, pp. 12, 56, 77, 86; Tony Duffy/Allsport, p. 13; Reuters/Marsh Starks/Archive Photos, p. 15; UPI/Corbis-Bettmann, pp. 16, 26, 27 (both), 28, 29, 33, 46; Reuters/Gary Caskey/Archive Photos, pp. 18-19; Doug Pensinger/Allsport, p. 22; Otto Greule/Allsport, pp. 24, 34, 61, 67; Jim Gund/Allsport, p. 31; Allsport, pp. 32, 83; SportsChrome East/West, p. 35; Al Bello/Allsport, pp. 37, 43, 68; Jonathan Daniel/Allsport, pp. 38, 78, 85; Andy Lyons/Allsport, pp. 40, 59; Reuters/Sue Ogrocki/Archive Photos, p. 42; SportsChrome East/West/Rich Kane, pp. 44, 96; Reuters/Ron Kuntz/Archive Photos, p. 48; SportsChrome East/West/Scott Brinegar, p. 52; Reuters/Bettmann, p. 54; Jamie Squire/Allsport, p. 58; J. D. Cuban/Allsport, p. 60; Archive Photos/Reuters/Kevin Lamarque, p. 62 (top); Reuters/Corbis-Bettmann, pp. 63, 75; Matthew Stockman/Allsport, p. 69; Reuters/Mike Blake/Archive Photos, p. 70; SportsChrome East/West/Vincent Manniello, p. 74; Zoran Milich/Allsport, p. 80; Reuters/Mike Blake/Archive Photos, p. 81; and Stephen Dunn/Allsport, p. 84.

Front cover photograph: © Mickey Pfleger/Sports California.